Mainly Scottish Steam

Mainly Scottish Steam

Thomas Middlemass

David & Charles : Newton Abbot

0 7153 6328 X

Set in 11/13 Linotype Plantin
and printed in Great Britain
by John Sherratt & Son Ltd.
at the St Ann's Press, Park Road, Altrincham, Cheshire WA14 5QQ
for David & Charles (Holdings) Limited
South Devon House   Newton Abbot   Devon

To my wife and daughters,
who understand

Contents

CONTENTS

8

List of Illustrations

PLATES

9

MAP

Introduction

A LOCAL bus plying in the Stirlingshire town of Falkirk exhibits on its destination screen LOCK 16. There was a time when Lock 16 was much more than the terminus of an urban bus route. In the pre-railway age the sixteenth lock on the Forth and Clyde canal, strategically placed in the middle of Scotland half way between the western and eastern seas, was a famous meeting place of land and water routes. Swift boats on the Glasgow–Edinburgh cross-country service passed deep-sea cargo vessels westbound with Baltic timber for the Clyde shipyards and ships outward bound to Hamburg with Glasgow-cured tobacco at Lock 16. In the fore-court of the Union Inn, adjoining the lock, stood the stage coaches ready to take the canal passengers to Stirling, Perth, Dundee and Aberdeen.

In the railway age Falkirk lost nothing of its fame as a meeting place of routes. The Edinburgh & Glasgow Railway was first in the field with its line passing along the hillside above the town. It was followed by the Scottish Central which took a diagonal course just to the west of the town and was to form a link in the chain of railways between Carlisle and Aberdeen. In 1865 the Edinburgh & Glasgow fell to the North British, and the Scottish Central to the Caledonian. These bitter rivals fought for supremacy in the Scottish heartland, pushing branch lines out to neighbouring towns and into the district's complex of foundries and factories.

Thomas Middlemass, the author of this book, is a London banker now. But when he first knew Falkirk as a schoolboy it

11

was throbbing with railway interest. The LNER and LMS were in command by then, but the place still teemed with North British and Caledonian engines as well as the newcomers from England.

Mr Middlemass conveys very well the fun of growing up in Falkirk in the 1920s and 1930s. With the family camera for company he sat in his favourite lineside spots for hours on end watching the trains go by. He haunted the local sheds, now and again pedalling his way on his bicycle to more remote sheds. Later, when he had a shilling or two to jingle in his pocket he ventured as far away as Glasgow and Edinburgh and Perth and Dundee, looking and recording all the time.

Every week-day just after school ended the Leeds Diner went flying through Falkirk High. That was an entertainment, especially when an NB Atlantic was in charge. There were Glens and Scotts to be seen on the Fifes and Edinburghs and Dunalastairs climbing up the bank from Grahamston to Polmont. Brand new Pacifics out of Hyde Park made fleeting appearances cutting their teeth on the Edinburgh–Glasgow slow trains. The Saturday after the second Monday of July was the Falkirk enthusiast's red letter day. That was the start of the Glasgow Fair when tens of thousands of Glaswegians poured out of their city by train— motors didn't matter then—and there were dawn to dusk processions heading east through Falkirk for Fife and the Lothians and through nearby Larbert for Aberdeen. Everything on wheels was out that day. Doubled-headed Aberdeen expresses passed the young observer's vantage point in a grand pageant, and down went details of the interesting pairings in his notebook; two Midland compounds, a compound and a Caley '60', a Jumbo and a 'Horwich'. One day he saw an old Jumbo leaving Larbert with a long Pullman car express—and he has a picture to prove it.

In this distinctive addition to railway literature the author has recaptured the delights and excitements of life as a railway enthusiast between the wars.

JOHN THOMAS

Acknowledgements

I AM indebted to Adam Martin for permission to publish the following photographs:

Pages 18, 35, 36 (top), 89, 143 (lower), 144 (lower).

All other plates are by the author. Grateful thanks are also due to K. J. Wynn, a young man without whose enthusiastic assistance many of the older photographs might never have seen the light of day and to John Thomas who has been a fount of both patience and knowledge.

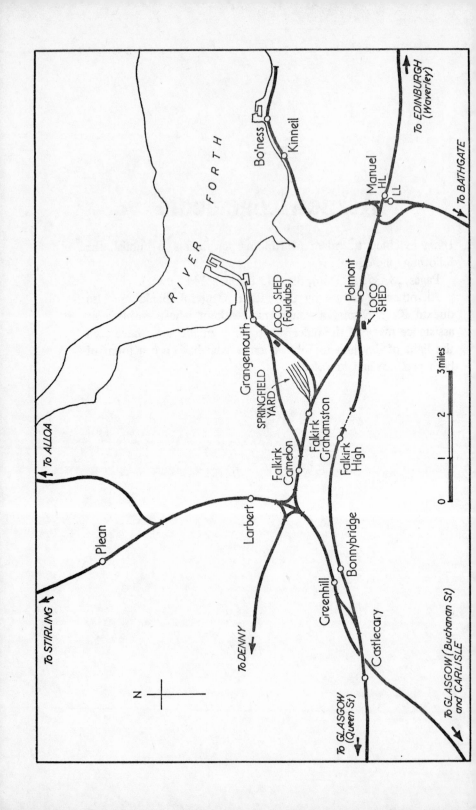

I

Falkirk—Centre of Operations

LOOKING back at railway life around Falkirk in the early 1930s it still seems remarkable that enthusiasts like myself were able to see almost every existing class of ex-NB and Caledonian locomotive without venturing further afield than the three main local stations—Falkirk High, Grahamston and Larbert. Even the few missing types could, I discovered in due course, be tracked down within a 25 mile radius of my home town. The reason for this was both simple and symptomatic of the weakness in Scotland's economy, for although the two major Scottish railway companies dominated territory ranging from Inverness and Fort Augustus in the north to Carlisle and Berwick in the south, the bulk of their motive power resided, as did most of the human population, in the central Scottish region.

Buried beneath the plethora of railway activity which enlivened Falkirk and district an almost more surprising fact lay concealed. The town supported two fair-sized engine sheds—one, LNER, at Polmont; the other, LMS, at Fouldubs—but of the combined locomotive studs only four were truly passenger machines. These were, ironically enough, humble 0-4-4 side tanks. One ex-NB pair worked the Grangemouth–Polmont–Bo'ness branch service, while the other, ex-Caledonian, pair performed similar duties between Larbert and Grangemouth. The rest of Falkirk's locos, fifty or so in number, handled freight traffic only.

A busy industrial town, supported largely by iron foundries and accommodating a population approaching 35,000, Falkirk held a commanding position south of the Forth estuary. Situated centrally on the narrow waist which separated Forth and Clyde, it was sufficiently removed from Edinburgh and Glasgow to have cocked a snook at both. Yet local culture, and certainly industrial allegiance, betrayed a distinct affinity with the west. Even our local dialect approached that of Glasgow in its spontaneity and generosity of expression, and, as townsfolk, we were accustomed to the grim consequence of having to depend on heavy industry. We understood the agonies of Clydeside when times were bad. No, Edinburgh as a city delighted me, but somehow, as a boy, I always felt Glasgow to be that little bit nearer.

THE EDINBURGH & GLASGOW RAILWAY

Historically, railway development at Falkirk marched with that of her great neighbours. In 1838 the Edinburgh & Glasgow Railway, first company in Scotland to construct what might be considered a real main line, set out to link the two cities. The company sought a straight and level route, and nearly accomplished its aim. There was only one drawback: the western approach, as planned, involved a descent of 1,450yd into Glasgow at an average drop of 1 in 45! Enterprising to a degree, the company accepted this formidable obstacle, laid plans to overcome it by provision of traction by cable and stationary engine, and bought the requisite ground at Cowlairs, then a rural spot on top of the incline. Not content with installing the all-important stationary engine, the E & G added foresight to confidence by setting down the foundation of Cowlairs's future carriage and locomotive works.

Teething troubles apart, their initiative paid dividends, for on 18 February 1842 trains began to run between Glasgow Queen Street and Haymarket. *Not* Edinburgh, it will be observed; for obtaining access to the city itself presented severer problems than had been envisaged. Latterly the immensely tough engineering task of boring Haymarket tunnel through solid rock proved too much for the schedule provided, and an extension of time was required. Strident objections meanwhile from powerful groups of Edinburgh citizens to the open passage of steam trains through the heart of the city were finally, and discreetly, overcome by the

page 17
LMS No 14605 (ex-CR No 51 of J. F. McIntosh's '55' class built at St Rollox in 1905) at Stirling in July 1936

page 18
LNER No 9906 *Teribus* (NBR Reid Atlantic No 906 built in 1911 by Robert Stephenson & Co Ltd) approaching Polmont at speed, on the 4pm Glasgow–Leeds express in August 1931

provision of yet another short tunnel through the Mound. Eventually, by the autumn of 1846 the last obstacle was breached, and through service was established between Glasgow and Edinburgh General station. For the first time in its history Falkirk, too, was on the railway map.

FALKIRK HIGH STATION

Granted a town in Falkirk's position could not justly have been ignored, E & G's recognition must have appeared to any stranger a shade cavalier, for Falkirk High station sat, remote and lonely, on a ridge a good mile from the centre of the town. This apparent slight, my father, an ex-NB railway goods guard, was always anxious to point out, was the legacy of a local landowner's refusal (long before the NB took over, of course!) to permit a more direct route through his property. Whatever else, I can vouch for the fact that a day spent at Falkirk High yielded not only a harvest of main line traffic, but a gloriously sunny, often windswept, panorama of the whole Forth valley into the bargain.

Along by Bantaskine bridge, a favourite spot where road, canal and rail converged, the western approach by rail to Falkirk High formed a natural amphitheatre. From here the view was superb. Falkirk's many foundries drew the eye, and there was no escaping the famous old works at Carron. Further east the matrix of Grangemouth docks was plainly visible, and the red bricks and water tower of the Caledonian shed at Fouldubs stood out clearly against their backcloth of ships, cranes and woodyards. From Grangemouth the coast line swept round grandly to Bo'ness, but hopes one might have entertained of glimpsing the mighty Forth rail bridge were thwarted by a perverse twist of the estuary. Nearer, but still a good mile distant, the sharp spine of Falkirk High Street reared, with its unchanging silhouette of steeples (the highest point and traditional focus of the town).

High station itself was remarkably unpretentious, with not even a bay to suggest the proximity of a large town. Nor were many passengers likely to be seen, for even the provision of a bus service early in the 1930s to alleviate the hardship of humping luggage to and from town by hand had failed, so far, to weaken the resolve of most Falkirk citizens to cling to the more conventional facilities of Grahamston station, situated so much more conveniently right in town. A few miles further east Polmont provided the necessary rail link between these two stations.

FALKIRK GRAHAMSTON STATION

I doubt if anywhere in Scotland one could have found a maze of metals more complexly operated than around Falkirk. With the sole exception of Falkirk High, which remained stoutly LNER, every other stretch of line locally was either owned by LMS, with running powers to LNER, or vice versa. Thus, though my family allegiance—loyally transferred en bloc with the NB to the LNER in 1923—remained basically unsullied we grew quite accustomed none the less to watching both major companies at work.

Grahamston station was a prime example of the dual role in practice. Owned by the LNER it nevertheless afforded open house to the LMS, and, indeed, provided the latter's sole access from Edinburgh to the north. From an LNER aspect it provided an alternative connection to Edinburgh, via Polmont, which spared citizens the long trudge by foot up to Falkirk High. To add to the confusion, and keep up with the LMS, it also offered equally chivalrous service to passengers bound direct for Glasgow Queen Street. Such trains ran west through Camelon, then, together with other LNER trains running direct from Stirling and Alloa to Glasgow, utilised running powers over LMS metals from Carmuirs junction, a little south of Larbert. At Greenhill LNER trains forsook the Caley main line to Buchanan Street, tiptoed gently up a spur through a small sleeper-creosoting yard, and regained access to Queen Street. Meanwhile, LMS trains at Larbert seeking Edinburgh used reciprocal running powers through Grahamston. Mostly express in nature, for the LNER already amply served the Falkirk–Edinburgh sector, their trains climbed up through Polmont, joined the LNER main line to Waverley, and enjoyed the privilege of using LNER metals all the way to Haymarket, where they hived off independently for Dalry Road and the Caley terminus at Princes Street. All very complicated, but delightful to watch.

Grahamston, in addition, was a veritable beehive of local branch activity, for both LNER and LMS liberated travellers from Grangemouth, a nearby landlocked industrial port, in all directions via Polmont/Bo'ness and Larbert. The four passenger tank engines I mentioned earlier were kept hard at it all day long. The LMS tanks shuttled to and fro, while the LNER engines were by the nature of things obliged to run round their trains at Grahamston. My own earliest memories just embrace the sight of one of Dugald Drummond's lovely little 4-4-0 tanks skipping thus round its two-coach NB train. How well I was to know its successors!

I am speaking of course of days before mass ownership of motor cars both widened and cheapened the concept of travel. A train journey then was an event, and as the bulk of my family's NB-orientated travel aimed east and south so, for my part, excitement began aboard the Polmont 'branch' at Grahamston station.

Most freight traffic generated locally emanated from Springfield, a large goods yard which commanded immediate access to Grahamston station; and from here goods trains were dispatched to all points of the Scottish compass. Winchburgh, Slamannan, Sauchton, Niddrie, Bathgate, Castlecary, Cadder, Alloa, Kipps —these were some of the names I grew up to hear as my father talked of his work.

LARBERT STATION

Larbert, situated on the outskirts of Falkirk, about eight miles south of Stirling, was the local LMS stronghold. In addition to swapping running powers with the LNER its importance lay in handling heavy traffic from Inverness, Aberdeen and Oban, which it then filtered towards Edinburgh through Grahamston, southward to London via Coatbridge, or simply direct to Glasgow Buchanan Street. Sole branch service was that to Grangemouth. Passenger traffic during holiday periods was particularly intensive, and well justified the provision of a spacious station which boasted of four running roads. Decades before, Larbert had played its part in the nightly drama which attended the Great Races to the North. It was comforting to think that some gallant blue Caledonian beauties must have streaked through there on their way to Aberdeen.

Larbert station, when I first knew it, was vintage Caledonian. My earliest view of the station was undoubtedly obtained from the open top deck of one of Falkirk's ancient tramcars; for my mother was wont to take us for a circular tram ride as a Sunday night treat. The trip, she reckoned in her own firm way, was exhilarating, cheap and health giving, provided one did not mind the noise. At one point of the tour the trams passed leisurely over Larbert station, so I, for one, did not mind the noise. Whatever I saw in the early days Royal blue must have featured large; and certainly 4-4-0s, for, where passenger work was concerned, the Caley, like their NB rivals, had grown to place great reliance on a fleet of simple robust inside-cylindered 4-4-0s. Not content with sharing this tradition, both companies brought to the 1923 grouping almost identical quantities of the type—just over 180 locomotives in each case.

By 1930 I, and such cronies as accompanied me, were visiting Larbert by bicycle, a form of increased mobility which encouraged us to spread our wings; thus our favourite haunts in that direction were more widely dispersed than in the Falkirk High area. Much the best viewpoint was the southern end of Larbert station itself. Here a steep grassy bank overlooked the platforms, and commanded a clear view of all traffic passing through. Eventual initiation into photography created fresh demands, but we quickly discovered that judicious movement along the embankment gave us a wide range of railway subject to choose from. We could photograph trains either standing at the platform, starting away, or making headway at not unreasonable speeds by a level crossing nearby. Even trains approaching from the south came within our compass, for very few were not booked to stop at Larbert, and this meant brakes were being firmly applied as the subject came within camera range. By comparison the Stirling end of the station was neither so well disposed to the sun, nor could if afford anything so flexible in the way of grandstand facilities.

It was at Larbert I took my first photographs of moving trains and in the process laid bare an interesting sidelight on my instinctively held theory that people talented musically were, by nature of their flair for rhythm, likely to be drawn to the steam engine.

As I was using a cheap box camera I had decided to release the shutter only when the engine had reached an ordained spot in the foreground. Only thus could I avoid the twin hazards of movement and ill focus.

For my first attempt the engine, a Dunalastair 4-4-0, being two cylindered, voiced a strong 1-2-3-4 impulse as she started from the station. All very well; indeed, to my mind all very musical—until the time came for me to release the shutter. To my astonishment I found myself completely incapable of depressing a small lever, simply because the slight mental effort involved had to be exerted *off* the first beat of the four impulse bars which had been hammering in my ears! I am sure, as I stood there trying to summon courage to perform my small duty, whilst the Dunalastair sailed past, I must have looked as foolish as I felt. Nor was it a fluke, for subsequent efforts evoked the same agonies of indecision. In years to come I learned painfully to segregate sound from vision, but the effort was never an easy one.

Perhaps my frailty thus exposed throws light on why odd unmechanical characters like myself feel so deeply for steam locomotives, yet remain unmoved by the sight and sound of diesel or electric propulsion.

2
Earliest Recollections

SOME people are born to be collectors. I was one, and two influences played their part in directing my energies towards railways. First, my father was a railwayman; second, I was lucky enough to spend my boyhood at a time when the steam locomotive still dominated land transport in this country. After grouping in 1923 four great companies waged fierce rivalry for public favour, and, blessedly free from many distractions which complicate life for youth today, I, and others, revelled in it. No question of pledging allegiance to Great Western or Southern arose. This should have left a simple choice. LMS or LNER? Yet, looking back now, I realise even that option was hardly mine to exercise; for the real ethos of railway rivalry was firmly handed down to me by my father who, in his capacity as a goods guard, served the North British Railway, and scorned the Caledonian Railway, with equal devotion.

'The Caley!' he would snort cheerfully, his pipe burning, his eyes rolling towards the ceiling, his statement unfinished. Like good railwaymen, my brother and I respected signals. We sat quietly. Presently would emerge some droll tale or other of hapless doings on the Caledonian. Father was particularly partial to World War I period, when Caley train crews sharing intensive freight in and out of Grangemouth docks relied perforce on NB conductors to guide them over strange territory. Dear old chap, how was he to know his quixotic semi-pugnacious loyalty would persist absurdly in his son's head long after both he and the NB had passed on, with the result that even in

24

1965 a trip north from London by west coast route could still evoke a mild twinge of self-reproof!

My father first saw light in 1870 at Duns, Berwickshire, and quit farm labouring as a young man to seek the comparative security of railway employment. He started as a junior porter at Leith Central, right in the heart of NB territory. By the time I arrived in 1917 he was firmly embroiled in the railways' war effort, and was stationed as a goods guard at Polmont junction, some five miles from our home in Falkirk. He was a tall, gentle, intelligent man, devoid of ambition and greatly devoted to his job. One could have sensed as much by glancing at a handsome mounted full plate photograph which formed, at the same time, one of his most treasured possessions and one of my earliest recollections. In it was depicted an early NB 0-6-0 goods locomotive, with paint and brasswork lovingly burnished. The driver and fireman were poised elegantly on the footplate. Below, at ground level, my father stood to attention, smartly uniformed, young and heavily moustached, his shunting pole held stiffly erect. A soldier could not have done his regiment more honour.

Men like him found no difficulty in equating an inborn inability to doff their caps with genuine pride at being 'a Company servant'. Pride in their job was the key, and certainly I knew it to persist all through my father's life. His duties as goods guard involved a great deal of shift work and lodging out, factors which must have played havoc with any attempt at normal family life; but I never heard a grumble from him, or my mother, on this score. Many cold dark winter mornings he must have trudged five miles down the permanent way from Polmont; yet I do not remember him ever dwelling on the subject.

On the contrary he took pleasure in passing on to us his love of railways and nothing delighted him more than an opportunity to exercise his right to a limited number of free passes annually, in addition to such privilege tickets as he could afford. This meant our family could economically visit a positive galaxy of relatives who worked on farms strewn over the Border country. Thanks to the tied cottage system farm labourers in those days had to be extremely mobile, and hardly a year passed without some relative or other moving on to fresh pastures. Father, however, was a determined man. He obviously drew refreshment from cultivating his country roots, and no matter how remotely an uncle or cousin contrived to bury himself in Border country, father and the LNER would find a way.

Cigarette cards, the *Wonder Book of Railways*, *Meccano Magazine*—all played progressive roles in stimulating my early interest in railways. I have no difficulty in recalling an official photograph of the new *Royal Scot* being published in the *Meccano Magazine* in 1927; nor do I forget the wrinkling of brows this massive new concept of locomotion caused in our (NB) household! At about this time a monthly publication called *Railways of the World* made its appearance. I used to rocket home from school the day it was delivered; usually, alas, to find my brother in prior possession. Next came sporadic copies of the *LNER Magazine*, gratefully received from a colleague of my fathers. Later, but infinitely more important, *Railway Magazine* followed from the same source.

My first journey by train involved a trip to Portobello, near Edinburgh. I must have been about five years old, which means I just managed to travel NB before it was too late. Portobello then to central Scotland was the equivalent of Southend to London. It offered a good cheap seaside holiday to thousands of working-class folk who could not have afforded to travel further afield, and during the holiday seasons, right up to 1939, an enormous volume of short-distance passenger traffic was handled there.

Even without father's partisanship I think I should have gravitated towards favouring the NB. Their vivid catalogue of passenger engine names apart, they made it so easy for one to be interested, through their distinctive habit of advertising a locomotive's alphabetical classification via a small cast plate on the cabside. At Springfield yard in the early days I saw quite elderly 0-6-0s, tender and saddletank, locomotives which did not as a class survive grouping very long. The names of Wheatley, Drummond and Holmes conveyed nothing to me at the time, but I saw some of the fruits of their craftsmanship, for I retain clear recollection, specifically of cabside plates lettered D and E, and generally of safety-valve mounted domes and rounded cabs. Aye, and four-wheeled tenders.

Even the playground of the primary school I first attended in 1923 offered a brief glimpse of the main line east of Grahamston. This was the year of the great regrouping and for a time it was still possible to spy flashes of rich NB ochre and the splendour of Caledonian blue. As far as the Caley is concerned, my earliest vivid memory recalls a Sunday school excursion to Stirling, ten miles distant.

Road transport, as we now know it, was hardly even then in its infancy, and when groups of people required moving, society thought automatically in terms of special trains. I embarked on this trip, fully prepared with the rest of the noisy juniors on board to enter into the spirit of the egg and spoon race, little realising what temptations lay ahead. Only when we steamed to our destination, and were marched to the chosen sports arena, King's Park football ground, did they reveal themselves. We found ourselves right alongside Stirling engine shed! I fear very little time elapsed before I abandoned thoughts of sporting fame in favour of much more exciting pursuits.

Clearly to this day I recall the cause of my undoing: the sight of a large locomotive, resplendent in Royal blue and shining brass, simmering and shimmering in the heat of a lovely summer's day. Probably a Dunalastair 4-4-0, whatever it was it hypnotised me, and in the process left a spell which was to remain potent for the rest of my life. I suppose I must have spent all afternoon sitting by the low fence quietly gaping at this beautiful machine. Eventually, I am told, my father succeeded in disengaging me. We walked back hand in hand across the field, and I remember I insisted on stopping from time to time to look back. For years after my father made great play of my 'defection' to the Caley; but I know that as he stopped with me at Stirling that day and patiently permitted yet another backward glance, even his stout NB heart must have warmed to that wonderful sight.

THE 1923 GROUPING

As my interest in railways gained momentum in adolescence so too did the pace of amalgamation. Locomotives seen previously in gamboge or Royal blue startled railwaymen by appearing in apple green and crimson lake. A new legend, LNER, began to be seen squeezed over new numbers on locomotive tenders, while one-time Caledonian engines sported huge five-digit numbers on tender or sidetank, with LMS blazoned against a red background on cabsides. The excitement of change could be felt in the air.

Transition, however, takes time, and many locomotives lingered on in original livery before the inevitable shop visit saw to their joining the new ranks. I remember seeing engines at Grahamston station still clinging tenaciously to NB colours and Caledonian blue. Gradually, their appearances became increasingly sporadic, until ultimately all appeared to have gone. The greater was our surprise when some time later an ancient outside-cylindered Caley 0-4-2 appeared on local branch duties, its one-time blue sadly faded, but still stubbornly announcing its origin. About this time the solitary Caledonian single wheeler also worked through Falkirk, but whether in blue or red I cannot recollect. Meanwhile, though rivalling each other in colouring their passenger locomotives the LNER and LMS at least reached common ground in deciding their respective quotas of goods engines should be painted black. A symbolic colour to match a sombre decision, ex-NB and Caley men no doubt felt. My father was scandalised at the time but, needless to say, learned to live with the impossible.

Oddly enough my sharpest memory of new LNER green remains with me in terms of one of the NB's smallest engines. We had gone through to Edinburgh, en route to Gifford, in Haddingtonshire, whence one of my father's relations had migrated. Waverley station, then as always, was a mighty busy place, but of the many locomotives which busied themselves about us my memory persists in isolating the tiny NB Drummond 4-4-0 tank which handled our Gifford train. These delightful little machines were a familiar sight on the network of branch lines which emanated from the east end of Waverley. Low boilered, with tall, elegant chimneys and solid-cast front bogies, they looked such sprightly morsels clad in their apple green. Facing no gradients in the course of their duties they could well afford to highstep daintily in and out of Edinburgh. Both passenger service to Gifford and 4-4-0 tanks vanished in the early 1930s, but I shall not readily forget my trip behind one of these little beauties.

NORTH EASTERN LOCOMOTIVES

About this time, too, I made my first acquaintance with North Eastern locomotives. The NB zealously guarded their right to handle all goods traffic and stopping passenger services to and from Berwick, but NE engines, nevertheless, by tradition ran express trains straight into Edinburgh. This privilege, no doubt thoroughly justified during the Great Races to the North, also bore the accolade of my father's approval. I could tell that by the tolerant way he allowed us to loiter at Waverley's east end, where the sight of an NE locomotive never failed to evoke from him some reference to Geordie. He was just as capable as the next (NB) man of telling tales of Geordie's occasional lapses in the past, but his anecdotes had an affectionate ring about them and we were not deceived. Woe betide, we well knew, any Caley man foolhardy enough to criticise the North Eastern in his presence!

First foreigners I saw, NE engines made a considerable impression on me. After the sturdy businesslike NB and Caley engines I had been used to, they seemed to my eyes positively flamboyant. Brass-lined splashers and gleaming boiler fittings, combining so beautifully with green livery, offered me a new and sophisticated concept in railway aesthetics. I liked what I saw.

Raven Atlantics made the deepest impression. Of great length, but somehow not massive, they were beautifully proportioned machines, seemingly born to their distinctive task of propelling East Coast expresses. They offered, too, a striking contrast to the NB Atlantics I already knew. In place of the Scottish engines' air of power and pugnacity, they displayed an elegance almost feminine in perfection; though femininity played little part in their performance, for they appeared to handle heavy loads quite effortlessly on the tough Edinburgh–Newcastle route, and this, too, without the pyrotechnics of the Reid Atlantics. My father would never have it that the climb through Penmanshiel was as gruelling to an engine as Falahill, on the Waverley route, but even he was quietly impressed at times to see a Geordie Atlantic calmly whirr through Cockburnspath, working hard, yet so quietly, at the head of a heavy southbound express.

After the symmetry of the Raven Atlantics the same designer's Pacifics were a strange mixture. I knew they existed but had not seen one, until one fine morning when father and two of his sons were walking near Burnmouth, in Berwickshire. The main line ran along the embankment above us, the sun was blazing, a train was signalled—all the ingredients of sheer bliss were present. In time we heard a train approach from Berwick direction. At first sight I guessed the engine was not an NE Atlantic, but I was hardly prepared for the astonishing sight of a Raven Pacific in full flight. I had never seen an engine like this before! The boiler, a straight barrel of enormous length, culminated in a typically roomy NE cab, the frame was not high, and bore three splashers on the midst of which gleamed the largest nameplate I had ever seen, bearing the legend *City of Kingston-upon-Hull*.

I still do not know which was the greater shock: my first sight of a Raven Pacific, or the suddenly imparted information that Hull, geographically speaking, was a mere abbreviation. Anyhow, the spectacle of that monster locomotive streaming past, gleaming green in brilliant sunshine, with her train of teak-coloured coaches, fairly silenced all three of us. Even father forbore his usual remark about Geordie. A little later a Raven Atlantic sailed past, and the spell was broken. Father pulled out his faithful old watch. 'Geordie's on time today', he observed, and watched the express disappear rapidly towards Berwick. 'Good engines these', he added approvingly. I smiled, and nodded my agreement.

LOCOMOTIVES ON EXHIBITION

That must have been about the time Gresley Pacifics were

introduced to Scotland. I distinctly remember changing platforms at Berwick at a time when the station was being rebuilt,
and in the process observing a Pacific without nameplates. A
much closer inspection was to come later, when we visited an
exhibition of rolling stock at Waverley station in 1928. The prize
exhibit was No 2563 *William Whitelaw*, complete with tunnel
tender and train of modern East Coast stock. The new non-stop
Flying Scotsman in fact.

Visitors were invited to board the train at the rear and walk
right through, via the corridor tender, to the footplate. Needing
no second bidding I scuttled through the train well ahead of my
father and brother, and thus enabled myself to loiter inside the
tunnelled tender, cheerfully pretending we were hurtling along
outside York and were due a change of train crew any moment.
Eventually my family caught up with me, and after thorough
inspection of the driver's controls I emerged from *William
Whitelaw*'s cab quite prepared to start all over again. We must
have been Border bound that afternoon for father firmly directed
me to the other exhibits and reminded me we had a train to catch.

The other locomotives on show remain clearly in my mind.
Gresley's new 4-4-0, 311 *Peebles-shire* was there, as were No
9595, ex-NB class N (LNER class D25), one of Gresley's recently
introduced J38 0-6-0s, and 2133 *Nettle*, a Sentinel-Cammell
self-contained steam coach, not long built and nicely finished in
green and cream. *Nettle* operated in the Edinburgh locality for
some time after, but the life of the species was comparatively short.

I was fortunate in being able to interest myself in railways in
the 1920s, else I should have missed seeing some lovely engines.
9595 was a case in point. She was one of a dozen 7ft coupled
express locos built by Matthew Holmes as far back as 1886.
Rebuilt later by Reid and clad now in gleaming green, she looked
so handsome that day at Waverley. In rebuilding, Reid had
retained the most satisfying aspects of Holmes's design—the high
twin splashers rising nearly to the boiler rail, the smokebox wings
with their graceful sweep, the long slender chimney narrowing
at its base—and had even improved her appearance by resiting the
safety valve behind the dome, and replacing the rounded cab, so

dear to Holmes, by a much more substantial side-windowed type. Here surely were the beginnings of the NB's new twentieth-century look.

The next locomotive I saw on exhibition carried its own story. The time was 1934, the place, Princes Street station, Edinburgh. Mounted unusually beneath the engine's conventional nameplate a much larger plaque conveyed information that she had been exhibited in Chicago in 1933 and, travelling with her train 11,194 miles over the North American continent, had been inspected by 3,021,861 people.

It was, of course, 6100 *Royal Scot*. Or was it? For if truth be known she and 6152 *The King's Dragoon Guardsman* exchanged identities in 1933—thus it was the latter locomotive which toured America and now appeared in public. No matter. I was unaware of the deception at the time but I very much doubt, so handsome was the pride of the LMS, if knowledge of the true facts would have reduced my pleasure at seeing her in the flesh.

How I discovered *Royal Scot* was to be exhibited at Edinburgh I shall never know. In 1933 there was precious little organised activity for railway enthusiasts; least of all in Scotland, where one ploughed a lone furrow indeed. But somehow the intelligence reached me, and I recall cycling through to Edinburgh for the purpose. My firm intention on reaching Princes Street station was to consume sandwiches in its quiet fastness before proceeding with the locomotive inspection. *Royal Scot* made nonsense of my plans, for the pangs of hunger vanished the moment I laid eyes on her.

The whole *Royal Scot* train had been deposited into one of the main terminal platforms. The locomotive herself was quite irresistible. She shone as though dipped in maroon enamel for the occasion, and her smokebox fittings, buffers and coupling rods gleamed as only burnished steel can. Quite overwhelmed, I stuffed my sandwiches in my pocket and joined the remarkably varied cross section of the public which queued at the wooden ramp connecting platform and cab. At footplate level Driver Gilbertson and Fireman Jackson, heroes of the *Royal Scot*'s North American exploits, held court and, looking a shade ill at ease in spotless overalls, patiently fenced with innumerable questions levelled at them by successive cab loads of visitors. Inside the crowded cab one's eye was arrested by an array of highly polished brass dials, and almost as soon as any one was touched by human hand the driver or fireman would apply his duster in reflex action.

Even in those days the variety of people who seemed drawn to steam was astonishing. One old lady at my elbow invited what was ostensibly her small nephew to finger the regulator and inquired sweetly in Edinburgh tones if this was 'the steering mechanism'. Driver Gilbertson it was who took the plunge, and I and others listened with cheerful and increasing fascination as the little lady slowly enmeshed the gallant driver in a hopeless cocoon of mechanical innocence. Poor Gilbertson, his brave but unavailing battle went on for some time; then mercifully Fireman Jackson took over while his colleague escaped. I followed him out, found him applying touches of oil about the cylinder and shyly requested his autograph. The look in his honest eyes as he handed back my book assured me that far from requiring sympathy he was enjoying a very proud day in his life.

With Fireman Jackson still heavily engaged on the footplate this seemed a propitious time to explore the train. It was beautifully appointed and offered spirited competition to the East Coast stock I held in such high esteem. The separate compartments, I remember, were panelled in various Empire (!) veneers, and each wall bore a neat plaque indicating the name of the wood and the geographical source of supply. I collected autographs en route from both fitter and guard, thus rearming myself with a grand excuse to revisit *Royal Scot*. Alas, by the time Fireman Jackson had obliged with his autograph valid reasons for paying subsequent visits to the footplate became rather difficult to invent.

When, after my fourth walk up the gangplank, I imagined I detected a flicker of recognition cross Driver Gilbertson's face, even I knew enough was enough—and, seeking out my bicycle, I set off home, thoroughly content with my day's work.

3

Springfield Goods Yard

IN the very early 1920s I lived almost within a stones throw of Springfield yard. Well known now as a refuge for preserved Scottish locos, Springfield then was a remarkable place where one could watch LNER and LMS engines pick their way fastidiously through joint freight operations. A level crossing bisected the yard and an iron footbridge offered excellent grandstand facilities.

The yard itself, though used jointly, was none the less clearly segregated. North of the footbridge was LMS territory, apart from odd LNER incursions to the local foundries and gas works, while in the southern half, which commanded access to the yard, LNER engines went about their business, content to ignore the occasional Caley arrival or departure. Hours spent on the bridge after school taught me that freight traffic was not so aimless as it seemed. I soon learned to anticipate three major evening events.

First was the departure of the LMS goods to Greenhill, nearest junction to us exclusively LMS. Punctually at 7pm every evening an ex-Caledonian Drummond 0-6-0 would descend tender first over the level crossing into the northern sector. There she would occupy herself performing shunting contortions, under such cramped conditions that the crossing gates had to be opened and closed several times. No one seemed to mind. Road traffic was negligible and pedestrians had merely to climb the footbridge, squeeze past a small boy on top, and coast down the other side.

Eventually, by 7.30 or thereabouts, the Drummond was ready. There she stood at the head of her train, fifteen wagons maybe and a van, squeezed up for lack of space to within feet of the

page 35
Known to the NBR as No 32, to the LNER as No 9032, to BR as 68113
and to the boys of Falkirk as 'the chipcart' a Holmes pug shunts at
Falkirk High while (*above*) ex-NER 4-4-2 No 714 passes on an
Edinburgh–Glasgow slow train in May 1929; and (*below*) LNER
No 2756 *Selkirkshire* approaches with a westbound train in August
1930

(*above*) LNER Director class 4-4-0 No 6384 *Edie Ochiltree* leaving
Falkirk High in July 1933; (*below*) Fife express leaving Falkirk in
June 1935 in charge of LNER 4-4-0 No 9242 *Glen Mamie*, NBR Glen
class, built in 1911

crossing gates, safety valves blowing, oil lamps flickering on buffer beam and cabside. If the night was darkening a vivid red glow from her firebox as the fireman stoked hard added urgency to the proceedings. I grant a small Drummond 0-6-0 may not rank high on anyone's list of impressive-looking engines but to me, watching aloft as the plot unfolded, the scene had all the magic of a main line departure.

Zero hour had its elements of drama. A salvo of telegraph bells in the signal box opposite would galvanise the keeper into thrusting and crashing a succession of heavy levers. I doubt at the time if I had the faintest idea what effect this was having, but I know I admired the man's dexterity tremendously. His next move was to throw open a window, thrust out a green flag and whistle up the train crew in a most urgent manner. Thence he was obliged to address himself to the more mundane task of winding the gates. Slowly, no matter how vigorously he applied himself, the two white gates came together. This done, he stood back. The rest was up to the train crew. Almost immediately a hoarse blast from the Drummond prefaced a noisy ricochet of buffers down the train, the guard's van was suddenly snatched into motion, and the Greenhill was on her way.

Straight away I became involved as the initial eruption of steam, smoke and grit from the Drummond's long chimney enveloped my vantage point on the bridge. This was the moment I had been waiting for. Somewhere in the midst of it all as a veritable volcano swirled about my head I would blissfully hold my ground, and listen intently to the beat of the Drummond as she started her way up the incline. Even without vision it was easy to tell when the last of her train passed below. Then as smoke gradually thinned I would again identify the Greenhill as her red tail lamp retreated up the yard. Slowly, painstakingly as she gained ground the turbulent scarlet glow crept on in the sky and gradually moved round towards Grahamston. Soon the engine disappeared off right and the tail lamp wound away from sight. Only then would it occur to a grubby, but happy, schoolboy on top of the bridge that going home had its attractions as well.

While all this was happening a less obvious, but more signifi-
cant, operation was taking shape in the LNER sector of the yard,
where a shunting engine was composing the nightly goods to
Carlisle. Its importance to me lay in the fact that many an
evening my father was to be its train guard. Although this was
an arduous duty involving thirty-six hours away from home it
was, I know, his favourite task. Like a similar duty to and from
Berwick it meant traversing his beloved Border country, an act
which though mostly accomplished in darkness in these circumstances never failed to delight him. While the Greenhill was still
fussing at the foot of the yard the wagons making up the Carlisle
goods were being quietly slipped up to a siding just beyond
Grahamston station. There they awaited the rather dignified
arrival, fresh from Polmont shed, of one of the NB's superheated
class S 0-6-0s.

In its completed state the train lay now a little back from a
road bridge which was in turn near the local library. Often when
my father was on duty I made a point of combining a visit to
the library with seeing the Carlisle off. She left about 8pm,
after the Greenhill had rumbled through in a westerly direction.

The knowledge that my father occupied the van made me long
to accompany him on his journey, but of course there was no
question of my being allowed to complicate his duties and I kept
my distance on the bridge. Soon the Carlisle got right of way
and with a sharp high-pitched NB whistle the superheater got easily
on the move. As she chuffed gently under the bridge my eyes
would focus hopefully on the guard's van. Father, however, was
a Scot and I understood his native distrust of demonstration.
Prolonged cheering and waving were out. His habit was to wait
until the van approached the bridge, lean out nonchalantly to
see if I were present, acknowledge my greeting with one wave
of his arm, and promptly retire inside. In view of what I considered to be the seriousness of his duties his gravity of manner
never seemed inappropriate. I thought he was wonderful.

So, of course, he was. Two mornings later he would reappear
at home, prepared to snatch a few hours rest before resuming
the same itinerary that evening. He liked to talk of his Carlisle

38

trips and in me he found a ready listener. So much did I absorb of his reminiscences that years later when he decided my brother and I should sample a trip to Carlisle by passenger train on the selfsame Waverley route no pilgrim to the Holy Land embarked on his journey with greater anticipation than I did.

The final departure from Springfield yard was, oddly enough, to be heard more often than seen, for the nightly goods to Berwick which my father also chaperoned periodically left after 11 pm. On the occasions I saw it the most I could discern in the near darkness was the headlamped and purposeful smokebox of the train engine, again a superheated 0-6-0, as she stood facing down the yard, her train behind her. Other nights I often lay in bed listening for the Berwick to leave.

Eventually the alert would come, a warning cockcrow from the superheater echoed immediately by the pilot at the top end of the train. A moment's pause, then as I strained to listen the two engines would take up their staccato duet in the still night as they reversed painfully up the severe bank. Ere long the bark of the pilot would soften as it receded into the distance, leaving the sole sharp voice of the superheater. Soon, quite drowsy now myself, I could hear even her bite lose edge as the heavy train won its way up the bank. On she pushed, softer and softer became her song. A few minutes later the silence of night was restored—for by that time not only the Berwick but usually I as well had succeeded in slipping into oblivion.

RAILWAYS AND FOOTBALL

Springfield yard was also the hub of a second branch of railway activity, football 'specials'. Football remains a favoured sport in Scotland, but in the days I talk of it amounted to a national obsession where male members of the populace were concerned. Consequently very few games in major league football failed to require railway excursion facilities. Indeed, when celebrated teams visited Falkirk several train loads of supporters rolled in with them. This practice had my wholehearted approval, for during the games the empty trains were mostly parked in Springfield yard whence they could be scrutinised from my vantage point on the bridge. The trains always faced away from me, thus the engines could not be immediately identified, but the sight of strangers in the camp was enough to whet my appetite. Details could be collected later on.

Like most Scots boys I enjoyed a football match, but lacked the funds to indulge. A little applied ingenuity soon solved that problem. While the crowds were assembling at the football ground I would be down at Springfield yard inspecting the special trains as they were stowed away empty. From a distance locomotive types could usually be determined, thus I learned well in advance if anything out of the ordinary was in the vicinity. Reconnaissance complete I would then make my way up to Falkirk's football ground, conveniently situated by the railwayside near Grahamston station. Then followed my conception of a pleasant Saturday afternoon.

From my perch by the lineside I was able not only to keep an eye on railway activities but could even share the excitement of the football match in a vicarious sort of way by allowing my imagination to respond to the 'Ohs' and 'Ahs' and roars of the crowd within. There, for an hour or so, I would sit, thoroughly content to await the cue for my next strategic move. This came ten minutes from the end of the game when the gates of the football ground were opened wide, the purpose of this exercise being to permit premature escape to patrons who wished to avoid the rigours of a mass exodus.

Alas, such is life, the poor fellows who had chosen what was ostensibly the line of least resistance found themselves nearly swept from their feet by a tidal wave, moving inexorably in the opposite direction, of local youngsters bent on seeing the last ten minutes of the match free of charge. I need hardly add my own spare frame was to be found in the thick of it. Once inside the ground the rest was easy; a quick check on the score and I was immediately absorbed in the remaining drama of the game.

When the final whistle went there was no need to hurry. I could afford to hold back from the stampede towards the exits, stroll out at leisure and simply cross to the railway bridge. Here I had a first-class view as the special trains approached Grahamston in turn, filled up with visiting supporters, and passed below on their return journey. Having collected details of each engine, all that remained for me to do was to nip home for tea, check my railway records, and for the remainder of the evening argue the merits of the football match with as great authority as if I had been present for the whole ninety minutes.

LNER football specials tended to be the prerogative of Scotts and Glens, with occasional help from unnamed 4-4-0s and ex-NB 0-6-0s. On the LMS side 4-4-0s likewise took the brunt, 0-6-0s shared, but compounds turned up latterly and even Caley class 60 4-6-0s were occasionally pressed into service. Then there was the memorable occasion—I can feel the excitement yet—when of all things a Caley 4-6-2 tank backed her empty football special down into Springfield yard. The incident must have taken place in the mid-1920s. I know I was very young and the engine was painted crimson lake. It was exciting enough from top of my favourite footbridge to watch the strange tank ease her coaches into a siding, but when she pulled forward light and proceeded to drop back slowly towards the level crossing I could hardly contain myself. The gatehouse keeper further confounded things by opening up, and I was still wondering why on earth a Caley 4-6-2 tank should want to visit the local gas works when the lovely red locomotive slid below the footbridge, passed the gates and halted at the water column beyond.

What a sight! In record time I dismounted and raced over to stand goggling as the fireman attended to the hose. Soon water welled from the sidetank and washed down an already immaculate crimson paintwork. The sun came out, and a burnished cut metal star in the centre of the Caley's smokebox fairly shone with pride. So wonderful was the spectacle a new and cogent anxiety leapt to my mind. Would she stay long enough for me to fetch my brother? For moments I hestitated, agonised by indecision, before deciding to risk all. Dashing 150yds up the street I found my brother reading quietly at home, yanked the poor astonished chap out, and raced him back down, trying the while, between gasps, to explain the purport of my apparent madness. Fortunately for me luck held. The Caley was still there and my brother was duly impressed.

Minutes later the gates swung shut and two pairs of appreciative eyes followed the tank as she made her way gently up the yard. Two hours later the same eyes were present on Grahamston bridge to witness her return her noisy load of football supporters back west.

Years elapsed before I was next to see a Caley 4-6-2 tank. 15351 it was, this time in her native habitat, Glasgow Central, and fulfilling her proper function at the head of a fast train to Wemyss Bay. Her crimson livery had gone, but even in black she still looked a model of neatness. Pacific tanks were never numerous in British railway design, but as I watched her depart briskly that afternoon here surely, I felt, was the trimmest of them all.

The only factor missing was the element of sheer magic which lingered on from that wonderful first appearance at Springfield yard years before.

4
Local Sheds

POLMONT shed features large in my memories as the base from which my father worked. Just beyond the west end of Polmont station the main LNER line from Edinburgh forked to permit two entries into Falkirk, and the tracks to Falkirk High promptly widened to accommodate a small marshalling yard. There, between yard and Union canal, stood Polmont locomotive depot. Polmont junction had assumed crucial freight importance during World War I, and the present shed, a large wooden structure, had replaced a much smaller NB one in 1919. It was well sited, and an enthusiast standing on the adjacent canal bank could see all that was going on. My first railway photograph, in fact, consisted of a view of Polmont engine shed.

As I look at the picture now I remember that Sunday morning in April 1934 so well. The sun shone brilliantly, reinforcing a sudden and ardent desire to try my hand at railway photography, and off I cycled with box camera slung over my shoulder. The assembly of motive power I unearthed at Polmont that morning was to remain fairly typical all through the 1930s, for of the thirty or so engines on shed it transpired that only three were not NB in origin.

Undoubted lord of the manor, and largest inhabitant, was 186, an LNER class K3 2-6-0. By now K3s had superseded NB superheaters on the Carlisle freight run and for many years 186 shared this duty with sister engine 191. Off duty one lodged at Polmont while the other rested at Carlisle Canal Basin shed. Later the same evening both would gird their loins for the return trip.

43

But though the two locomotives spent their lodging time alternating evenly between sheds, 186 was regarded as the Polmont engine, and as such her constantly immaculate condition was a credit to the shed. Being in addition 'my father's engine'—or so it seemed from the proprietary nature of that stalwart's conversation—she acquired particular lustre in my youthful eyes. Even now, forty years later, the sight of number 186 on car registration plate or lottery ticket never fails to trigger off the happiest of memories.

The two other foreigners at Polmont were strange intruders, class J9 0-6-0s, viewed by us as ex-Great Central locomotives, but relics actually of the Manchester, Sheffield & Lincolnshire Railway before that concern was renamed Great Central in 1897. Why they should have been imported into an area already richly endowed with sturdy NB 0-6-0s I could never understand. Nevertheless, during their years at Polmont Nos 5661 and 5666 performed a deal of donkey work, mostly around Springfield yard. A little later, to our astonishment, they were supplemented in these duties by a brace of ex-Great Eastern J69 0-6-0 tanks, Nos 7347 and 7368. The GC engines looked odd enough in our eyes, though they had in the last analysis a not unpleasing lean rangy look about them, but the Great Eastern tanks, with their absurd squashed appearance and rimless stovepipe chimneys, really took some swallowing. I doubt if my father ever became quite reconciled to their presence; though we could hardly visit Grahamston station without finding one or the other pottering about in the vicinity. Still, they too were nicely maintained, and in their own way made quite a gallant picture as they dashed back and forth, breathlessly intent on detaching a coach or sneaking a few wagons down to Springfield.

NATIVE STOCK AT POLMONT

The bulk of Polmont's remaining occupants were 0-6-0 tender locomotives, with emphasis on J36s, or ex-NB class C as we preferred to know them. NB cabside plates had not been removed after grouping, so the old classifications lived on and LNER-styled Js 35, 36 and 37 remained B, C and S in Scottish eyes. The Cs,

LOCAL SHEDS

like Caley Drummond 0-6-0s, were astonishing examples of the durability of Scottish locomotive design. Shopped originally by Holmes in 1888, and rebuilt subsequently by Reid, they had carried the brunt of NB freight activity over a widely varying system for fifty years and had still contrived to survive more or less intact as a class.

In 1934, somehow, we did not think in terms of locos being scrapped, but I doubt if pressed to it I could have guessed that some of these Cs would put in another thirty years' hard labour before surrendering to Cowlairs. There must have been a dozen of them at Polmont, all occupied daily on the labyrinth of mineral traffic duties which existed in the area. *Somme, Allenby* and *Plumer* were the only named residents. Occasionally we had a visit from *Maude* and *Byng*, but Polmont was not greatly addicted to receiving visitors—in locomotive form I mean. An odd freight engine from foreign parts might stay overnight but, that apart, water columns and turntable facilities for some of the more involved Glasgow–Falkirk passenger workings were the sole attraction.

Next in line, and more powerful than the Cs, were the Bs, introduced in 1906 by Reid, Holmes's successor. Provision of a larger boiler, with corresponding rise in pressure to 180lb, had necessitated a shortened chimney and dome. This gave the B class a much more sophisticated look. The three or four shedded at Polmont were employed on goods traffic slightly superior to that handled by the Cs.

Finally came the pride of the NB, freightwise at least. These were Reid's ultimate in 0-6-0s, his S class, introduced in 1914 as superheated developments of the B. Fine, handsome locos they were, too. These were the engines which had for so long taken the load on the tough Carlisle and Berwick routes, where their soft, rather lazy exhaust tended to deceive. It could assume real bite when conditions warranted.

The half-dozen locomotives remaining at Polmont were tanks. Two were class A 0-6-2s, sturdy machines of 1920 vintage built expressly for marshalling-yard duties. The Polmont pair, 9391 and 9523, were invariably to be found working at Springfield.

45

Despite their unassuming appearance they were interesting engines—and certainly deceptive—for their long NB chimneys, low-pitched boilers, small, nearly flat-roofed, cabs and 4ft 6in driving wheels gave little hint that in their prime they had rejoiced in the role of being the NB's most powerful freight locomotive.

Herein lies an odd tale of alphabetical misfortune. Latterly only Reid's 0-6-0 superheaters succeeded in outpowering his 0-6-2 tanks. Unfortunately, as the latter already occupied pride of freight place at class A, the poor superheaters had to be content with a place at S; not only bottom of the NB list, but positioned into the bargain behind the most modestly powered class of NB passenger tank.

Two more Polmont inmates were solitary passenger tanks, class M 0-4-4s, whose duty it was to maintain local branch service between Grangemouth and Bo'ness. Following on the heels of Drummond's little 4-4-0 tanks this brace of sturdier Reid locos, 9259 and 9350, class G9, vintage 1909, arrived at Polmont in 1925 and spent the next ten years of their lives toiling locally. Though only propelling two coaches they had to face many times daily the severe climb from sea level to Polmont. The resultant mechanical wear and tear may explain in part why the class, never large in number, disappeared unusually early for NB locomotives; though the process was undoubtedly hastened by the influx into the Glasgow area of Gresley's new V1 2-6-2 tanks. This had the effect of releasing a number of NB 4-4-2 tanks for branch line duties all over the NB system, and by 1935 two Atlantic tanks had quietly taken over at Polmont. The 0-4-4 tanks, equally quietly, vanished.

Last, and I am afraid least, came two G class 0-4-0 saddle tanks, class Y9 under LNER auspices. Holmes designed, and dating back to 1882, these little engines, with their tiny wheelbase, were primarily intended for dock work. Some, but not the two at Polmont, had wooden tenders permanently attached. With 3ft 8in driving wheels and square wooden buffers the saddle tanks presented an odd sight as they paddled light along the main line each day, en route to their duties at Falkirk High and

Castlecary brickworks. A peculiar dipping and weaving motion, generated when speed ventured to exceed 10mph, earned them the rather irreverent title of 'chipcart'; a cruel accuracy, I fear, like so many youthful observations. In fairness to the men at Polmont, however, it should be recorded that 9032 and her sister 9010 were kept in splendid condition. It might also be recorded that I would not have dared use the expression 'chipcart' in my father's presence.

FOULDUBS SHED

Years before, when I was a very small boy playing in a public park, I used to be tantalised nightly by the strange behaviour of a Caledonian 0-6-0 tank. Her habit consisted of proceeding almost to the top of the Grangemouth branch line, pausing awhile, then reversing back down whence she came. At that age the unconventional nature of such railway conduct worried me little. What did intrigue me was the odd basketlike arrangement she sported on her chimney. Later I learned that this was spark-arrester equipment, considered necessary for locomotives working all day in timber-strewn dockland. The dockland in question was Grangemouth and the tank was domiciled at Fouldubs, the Caley equivalent of Polmont shed. Although I was to pass the shed often, not until I embarked on railway photography did I make a close inspection of Fouldubs.

Again the occasion was a Sunday morning. As I wandered round, the close affinity between the rival sheds soon became apparent. Apart from the fact that Polmont was a through-running shed while Fouldubs was terminal, they shared most other things in common. Each sheltered three native types of 0-6-0 tender engine developed from late nineteenth-century prototypes, each contributed two solitary passenger locomotives in the form of 0-4-4 tanks, each shed had five running roads and roughly the same number of inhabitants. Above all, ten years after grouping each depot was still steeped in the tradition of its old parent company. Obviously the minds of NB and Caledonian men were as indestructible as their locomotives.

Fouldubs had even fewer foreigners than Polmont: only two

47

LMS class 4F 0-6-0s. These were an early post-grouping development of Fowler's well-known Midland design, with boiler mountings reduced to meet northern operational requirements. Extremely handsome engines, they had been built by the hundred and could be found all over the LMS system. Like Polmont, however, Fouldubs was already well equipped with reliable 0-6-0s, and a very small quota of Fowlers sufficed.

Caledonian maids of all work were Drummond's celebrated Standard Goods 0-6-0s, known affectionately in later life as 'Jumbos'. More numerous than any NB 0-6-0 class they operated all over the Caley network. Quite a number were fitted with vacuum brake and cheerfully worked passenger or freight as circumstances required. Fouldubs had a dozen of them, no doubt a mixture of Drummond, Lambie and McIntosh products. I remember observing that one of the oldest retained still its wooden tool box, behind the tender on the rear buffer beam. Another, 17362, continued to blazon her identity in large numerals on her tender long after general practice had restored numbers to the cabside. Yet another, 17274, betrayed her early Drummond parentage by the underslung springs her tender bore. A tendency to foul lineside objects obliged Drummond to abandon this practice early in his career. None of the Caley 0-6-0s I saw at Fouldubs carried a spark arrester, for the work of dock shunting was effected exclusively by tank locomotives. In those days, too, all sported the original tall Caledonian chimney. Mercifully we had no premonition of the wretched stovepipes they were to inherit at the hands of British Railways.

The Drummonds had been graded by the LMS at 2F. At class 3F came their McIntosh successors of 1899, two of which were stabled at Fouldubs. Though retaining something of the Drummond lines, these were much more substantial-looking machines, strongly resembling in appearance the NB class C 0-6-0s as rebuilt by Reid. Gradually, on both NB and Caledonian, the flowing slender creations of Drummond bowed the knee perforce to a more purposeful modern look, and this evolution was most marked in the final superheated 0-6-0 designs of both companies. Fouldubs had a couple of the Pickersgill variety. Like all the latter's contributions to Caley motive power they were easily identified by their one-piece chimney and generally robust appearance.

The rest of Fouldubs's family were sidetanks. The two 0-4-4 tanks there, 15129 and 15142, stayed their branch line course much longer than did their NB equivalents. There was a brief spell when the LMS chose to experiment with a maroon-coloured Sentinel-Cammell steam coach between Larbert and Grangemouth—I have a picture of 29910 at Larbert, taken in July 1934—but presumably the daily uphill grind proved too much for her, for the tanks soon returned. They were to remain in command for a long time to come.

The other tanks were 0-6-0s, associated with shunting duties at Grangemouth docks and mostly all equipped with spark arresters. Two, 16152 and 16164, were small, dainty McIntosh creations of 1911 origin; humble engines which bore an odd distinction, for they were the only outside-cylindered design produced by McIntosh. Further down the Forth a very similar type of Reid NB tank was employed at Bo'ness docks.

Fouldubs's locomotive stud was rounded off by half a dozen sturdy McIntosh inside-cylindered 0-6-0 tanks. These extremely solid-looking engines spent their days shunting tirelessly round Grangemouth docks, and were not known to venture far from base. I am reminded by a photograph of one that colour film would have been a boon to enthusiasts in those days. For No 16300 carried a number plate on her smokebox, Midland style, and her train crew had painted the numerals startlingly white against a bright red background. Quite often amongst Scottish engines one came across decorative expressions of pride and affection on the part of enginemen. Some of the stars and figurations which appeared, cut in shining metal, on smokebox centres must have taken considerable skill and patience to produce. Where identity was concerned not many Caley locomotives carried number plates in front, and considering Caley buffer beams were red-painted blanks, as opposed to neatly numbered NB beams, identification of a Caley engine (after being photographed) passing at speed sometimes posed tricky problems.

FOULDUBS'S DISTINGUISHED GUEST

Football specials for Wembley, required bi-annually, denuded almost every nook and cranny in Scotland. The one nearest and dearest to me started from Grangemouth and ran under LMS auspices. In the mid-1930s Caley 4-4-0s began to yield such duties to Compounds; though sometimes one of each would handle the train, which was always double headed. A stirring sight it made, too, as it thundered and sparked its way up from Grangemouth. Entry into Grahamston station was positively gladiatorial as Falkirk's tartaned legions surged forward to claim such seats as remained. Then one year, 1938 to be precise, a remarkable thing happened.

As usual I had seen the Wembley special off, but her return trip had a habit of decanting supporters at such an early hour at Grahamston that I was never present to witness the scene. This Sunday morning, however, my friend Adam, whom I shall introduce presently, and whose house afforded a snatched view of the Grahamston line, brought me electrifying news. Not only had a Royal Scot brought in the special, but rumour had it she was resting right now at Fouldubs shed.

A Royal Scot at *Fouldubs*! Frankly, I informed Adam, I doubted it. Still, in the process of waxing sceptical I took the precaution of borrowing the family bicycle. Off we pedalled, first stop, Fouldubs. No sign of a Royal Scot at first sight. Undaunted, if a little dismayed, we employed the devious approach usually called for if we thought the shed inhabited. The coaling stage came into view. Adam was right! For there, in broad daylight, stood the first passenger tender engine we had ever seen at Fouldubs. And what an engine—6122 *Royal Ulster Rifleman*! Of course, in my excitement I had completely forgotten to bring my camera. Fortunately Adam's father showed more presence of mind, and turned up latterly to record the scene. Of such things are immortal memories made.

5
Local Traffic

THE LNER Glasgow–Edinburgh main line became an integral part of my life from the time I graduated to Falkirk High School in the autumn of 1928. In class we could hear the trains as they passed, half a mile away. School dinners had not yet been invented and I soon badgered my mother into letting me take sandwiches for lunch rather than come home, so that I could spend my lunch hour up at Falkirk High. It meant, of course, seeing the same few trains day in, day out. That gave no cause for worry; weekend observation would attend to the gaps.

Saturday mornings found me up bright and early. If the family bicycle was available Larbert might be my objective; if not, the sooner the tramp up to Falkirk High got under way the better. My mother, dear woman, would make sandwiches, knowing I would be missing for the rest of the day, and these plus a bottle of 'pop' would sustain me until I returned home of an evening in the usual schoolboy's state of ravenous hunger. One liked company on these day-long vigils, and invariably my accomplice was one, Adam Martin by name, now a respectable BSc living in Kent. All through boyhood and adolescence Adam and I doggedly pursued joint interests in music and railways. His father, a kindly man and keen amateur photographer, later gave us much encouragement and assistance in our early efforts at railway photography.

FALKIRK HIGH STATION
Along by Bantaskine bridge Adam and I would sit happily

51

for hours on end, thoroughly conversant with train schedules, and fully competent to occupy ourselves with harmless mischief during periods of railway inactivity. The variety of locomotives operating passenger traffic through Falkirk High at that time was sheer bliss, and engine names sprang so profusely from both NB and LNER sources as to gladden the heart of any schoolboy.

Directors and Shires had succeeded by 1928 in wresting the pick of Edinburgh–Glasgow express traffic from NB locomotives, except for the odd intervention by Reid Atlantics. Scotts, unabashed and lively as ever, clung more tightly to their privileged position at the head of Fife trains and otherwise contented themselves with handling what main line traffic remained. Their partners, the Glens, ever mindful of their original west of Scotland mission in life, still preferred to concentrate on duties rostered from Glasgow. The way we saw it, however the LNER chose to permute their locomotives—nine trains out of ten passing through Falkirk High still had named engines at their head. Thus during the tender years was evolved our marked preference for haunting Falkirk High rather than Larbert.

Fortunately evolution is a continuing process. Just as my own father had handed on to me an abiding love for the steam engine Adam's father planted in my mind the desirability of recording the beauty and dignity of its passing. His own interest in photography took him back to World War I, but it was not until the late 1920s that the combined enthusiasms of his son and myself persuaded him to consider the railway engine as a subject. He not only loved it, but passed on the 'bug'.

The earliest Falkirk High study I can summon is one of his: that of 714, an NE C7 Atlantic, at the head of the 3.15 stopping train to Glasgow Queen Street. May 1929—heavens, was it *forty*-odd years ago! The condition of the Atlantic speaks for itself. Rich green livery, opulent lining, polished brass beadings; not unusual features in those days, they spelt simply 'railway pride'. A brace of these beauties, ousted from East Coast duties by the advent of Gresley's Pacifics, worked through Falkirk High for the best part of a year. Actually, time for both NE and NB Atlantics was running shorter than we realised, for in June 1930

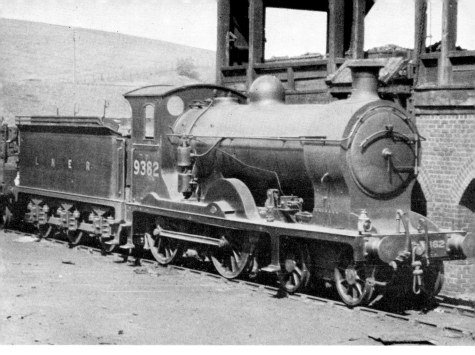

page 53
(*above*) LNER No 9382, completed as one of Reid's second 'Intermediate' class in January 1910, at Eastfield in June 1935; (*below*) Holmes NBR No 786 (LNER No 9786) built in 1900 is shown here as re-built by Reid in 1919 at Polmont in July 1934

In this picture taken at Larbert in July 1935 the photographer has captured Pickersgill's first 4-6-0
design and his last 4-4-0 for the Caledonian. LMS No 14497 (*left*) was completed by the North British
Locomotive Company in 1922 as CR No 66. The train engine on the Glasgow–Aberdeen express is
No 14630 built by the LMS in 1925 to the Caledonian design of 1916. The pilot is Midland com-

astounding news reached our ears. A Gresley Pacific had been seen at Falkirk High!

I smile as I recall the alacrity with which Adam, his father and myself got up to Falkirk High at the first available opportunity, and warm yet to the memory of *William Whitelaw* as she drifted in with immense casual dignity on a stopping train to Glasgow. Gresley Pacifics on their own stamping ground were one thing, but the sudden apparition of this great graceful machine in *local* surroundings had what I can only describe as an epoch-making quality. While Adam and I gaped, his father busied himself with camera and tripod, then sailed off home by bicycle. We followed by foot and by the time we reached Adam's house the developed plate, still wet, was triumphantly ready for inspection.

THE EFFECTS OF AMALGAMATION

Even by 1930 anyone caring to take an interest could still savour much of the old NB atmosphere, for only really elderly specimens of locomotive and rolling stock had been pensioned off. NB men's reaction, too, to grouping had been constructive, and early policy about locomotive colouring had been interpreted so enthusiastically that all NB passenger engines, tender and tank alike, had been given their coat of apple green paint. Poor NB men—their exuberance, and mine, took a nasty tumble when economies imposed in 1928 ordained that, in future, of all NB locomotives only Atlantics would qualify for green livery. The Reid engines earned their distinction, for right to their dying days they were beautifully maintained by Scottish enginemen. Symbolic, too, of lingering company pride, which the Gresley régime, wisely, did nothing to discourage, NB men clung determinedly to the small metal class plates on the cab sides of their locomotives. The plates were, of course, hopelessly irrelevant, but even when events of 1928 caused loco numbers to be transferred from tender to cabside the resultant congestion thereon was simply resolved by removing the NB plates and resiting them a little higher up the cabsheet!

One long standing NB domestic practice, that of employing

locomotive headboards, was even taken up and further developed by the LNER. So accustomed were we to see NB passenger trains advertise their destination by means of the tidy, curved boards the locos carried on top of their smokeboxes—with the words CRAIL, EDINBURGH, etc, blocked in white on red background— we hardly even noticed a gradual LNER transition to black lettering on a white background. Next the LNER fitted title-boards along the coach roofs of their expresses. By 1931 modern practice had evolved, and ex-NB men could derive quiet satisfaction from seeing the 10am express leave Waverley behind a Gresley Pacific whose smokebox supported a deep white curved headboard bearing the legend FLYING SCOTSMAN.

NAMED TRAINS

Inter-company rivalries of the 1930s also produced spirited competition in the art of naming express trains. Falkirk High had its share. Probably its most distinguished visitor was the *Queen of Scots,* that lovely train of brown and cream Pullman cars which plied between London and Glasgow. The up *Queen* left Queen Street at 10.15am, and lost little time covering the 21¾ miles to Falkirk. The task of hauling a train of such modest length and weight admirably suited a 4-4-0, none more so than the big Directors of 1924, and the sight of *Flora McIvor,* or other of her compatriots, streaming along the high straight towards Falkirk High, shining in lined black livery at the head of seven Pullman cars, had a nobility which lifted the heart. The northbound *Queen* left Falkirk High just after 8pm and dusk lent even greater enchantment to her passing; for, inside her, the spectacle of passengers seated at dinner, the soft light of table-lamps enhancing snowy linen and shining cutlery, and attendants gravely going about their business, added magic to a formality which, for us, belonged to another world.

The Pullman offered dignity, but the event we held in highest esteem was the Glasgow–Leeds express tearing through at 4pm. The Leeds was one of few which did not stop at Falkirk High. We knew it ran to a fast schedule and from the moment she was signalled the pleasurable anticipation of watching for her in the distance generated its own excitement. In early days she was liable to be hauled by either Reid Atlantic, Shire or Director. An equally warm place should have been reserved in our affections for the morning Glasgow connection with the *Flying Scotsman* had not her scheduled stop at Falkirk High obliged her to approach the station in much less dramatic fashion.

These, too, were the days when Gullane and North Berwick were sufficiently fashionable holiday resorts to merit a special daily service from Glasgow, known as the *Lothian Coast Express*. To this train was attached the only other Pullman car we saw at Falkirk High. Again a Director usually performed, but the Pullman car, jammed on this occasion between NB stock, sadly lost all semblance of dignity.

ROLLING STOCK

I fear NB passenger coaches had a high, wide and unhandsome look which even I could not relish. The trouble stemmed mainly from the flattish semi-elliptical roofs the company favoured. Looking more like chariots, coach roofs bore rows of long spiked lamp necks, and their high, straight sides were liberally blistered with duckets and vents, some of them not even functional. The only rakish vehicle I ever saw on the NB was a six-wheeled newspaper van which used to whirl back and forth between Edinburgh and Glasgow at the tail end of passenger trains, flaunting externally the brightly coloured insignia of *The Scotsman*, Edinburgh's national daily newspaper. As for NB upholstery, that could be really spartan at times. I still retain painful memories of bouncing up and down to Polmont on firmly stuffed seats whose long needles of horse hair emerged to play havoc with the backs of my bare knees!

Still, the LNER utilised the multivaried rolling stock it inherited much more flexibly than did the LMS, and soon their central Scottish trains, once dourly NB in make-up, began to assume quite a cosmopolitan character. Ex-NE coaches, easily recognised by their clerestory roofs, made increasing appearances around Falkirk High, and were reinforced before long by GE stock, sometimes even by an odd maroon M & NB stray from the Waverley route. Then, when a regular through service between Aberdeen and Penzance was switched in the early 1930s to link Glasgow and Penzance instead, to our daydreams was added the excitement of seeing a GWR coach pass daily through Falkirk. I used to watch the long chocolate and cream carriage glide through the station, and sigh at the miscellany of unfamiliar English names strung along its destination board—BANBURY, WESTBURY, PENZANCE. How more deeply might I have sighed had I guessed that, deep down in Wiltshire, a little girl living in Westbury also saw the through coaches pass her home daily—and was destined to become my wife before the next ten years were out!

LOCOMOTIVE SURPRISES

Around Falkirk locomotive surprises were never far away. In 1924 the twenty-four new Director 4-4-0s supplied in the main by Kitson & Co of Leeds at Gresley's instigation played a prominent part in my early railway education; for most of them, when new, were 'run in' on a convenient Glasgow–Falkirk turn. The train, known to us as the 'Dinner time', employed the line which could be seen from my primary school playground. It made a leisurely appearance in and out of Grahamston station, and the distant sight of a new engine going in encouraged us to scamper up from school during lunch break to collect the name safely second time round. These were exciting times, for not only were the massive green Directors completely strange to us, but they too carried names borrowed from Sir Walter Scott. All in the best NB tradition!

The Directors were a great success in Scotland. They offered welcome relief to the hard-pressed Scotts, and soon gained a near monopoly on heavy traffic between Edinburgh and Glasgow. Even the combined advent in 1927 of Shires and Pacifics failed to deprive them of a justly earned share of the best work, and their distinctive steely crunch as they got to grips with a train from a standing start at Falkirk High remained as music to my ears right up to the war years.

The 'Dinner time' was as big a success, for in 1928 the first ten Sandringham 4-6-0s, destined for East Anglia though built in

Glasgow, were also 'run in' through Falkirk. *Sandringham, Audley End, Burnham Thorpe*—we picked them off one by one, almost delirious with excitement, not knowing whether to thank the LNER or NB Locomotive Co for our unexpected daily blessing. In 1931 similar good fortune came our way when Gresley introduced a further eight Shire 4-4-0s, commencing No 2753 *Cheshire*. This batch anticipated later LNER standard practice by appearing fresh from the shops with number painted prominently on the cabside. Only the letters LNER remained on the tender.

Talking of Shires, one Saturday morning in August 1930 found Adam and I east of Polmont station, gazing fixedly at a locomotive which had just brought in the 10.14am from Queen Street. We had dismissed her as 'just another Shire', until a second look as she faced us in the distance jolted us into realisation that no Shire *we* had ever seen carried *steam pipes*! We looked blankly at each other, and what had looked like being an ordinary Saturday morning began to sizzle with excitement. After what seemed to be an interminable delay the Shire made a move. She approached, and we waited tensely; Adam crouched over his camera, I, charged with the task of identifying the strange object, pointing like a retriever. The locomotive passed, Adam looked up. '346 *Buckinghamshire*', I reported in awed tones, and added rather feebly, 'The outside valve gear was different'. It was different all right, for Gresley had decided to experiment with rotary cam Lentz motion and here, did we but know it, was the precursor of the later Hunt class. For a long time that one solitary English Shire remained, enigmatically segregated, in our notebooks.

Another day in 1935 I was labouring uphill towards Falkirk High, and nearly fell from my bicycle when a GE Holden 4-6-0, Glasgow bound, thrust its gaunt outline across my horizon. I had met 'Hikers' the year before at Liverpool Street, but as always the sight of the unfamiliar in *local* surroundings carried unforgettable impact. A couple of these engines worked between Edinburgh and Glasgow for some time, then vanished. Next we heard they were coping successfully north of Aberdeen.

We were aware, too, that a dozen or so ex-GN K2 2-6-0s had been named after Scottish lochs by their designer, Gresley, and transferred to Eastfield for West Highland duties. The knowledge did not lessen our joy when one afternoon in July 1935 4700 *Loch Lomond* put in a rare appearance at Falkirk High, heading a Glasgow Fair special. Ah, yes, great days!

FALKIRK GRAHAMSTON STATION

Grahamston station, despite its comparatively modest pretensions, also developed a useful penchant over the years for springing new types on us. The earliest 'foreigners' I saw there must have been LMS Standard 0-6-0s when early in the 1920s they slipped in place of Caley Pickersgill 0-6-0s at the head of a goods train which passed nightly through Falkirk, going west, known to us as the 'Aberdeen Goods'. Some years later the same train provided us with our first astonishing sight of a Horwich 2-6-0. There was also a minor LNER service between Edinburgh and Larbert, a matter of a couple of trains daily each way, which managed to employ a remarkable sequence of secondary class locomotives. I can recall two rebuilt Holmes 7ft 4-4-0s, 9595 and 9596, green and incorrigibly handsome, engaged thus in the closing years of their lives. Then Holmes 6ft 6in 4-4-0s, D31, took over, to share duties subsequently with a miscellany of other NB 4-4-0 types, named and unnamed.

I am sure the 'Larbert' must have been a spare engine turn, for one never knew from day to day what to expect. Nevertheless, the sudden appearance thereon one fine evening of a GN 4-4-0 seemed to me to savour slightly, however blissfully, of the ridiculous! Gresley, always possessed of a generous regard for other designers' locomotives, had dispatched all fifteen class D1s, built by Ivatt in 1911, north, with boiler mountings suitably reduced, to hold the fort while the Scottish Directors were being built. Quite a number in their time worked through Grahamston, and once we had absorbed the initial shock of their shaped, but windowless, Ivatt cabs we grew to admire No 3061 and company. My last recollection of D1s is of witnessing 3064 one post-war day near Haymarket, doughtily charging on, with *Haystoun of Bucklaw* behind, at the head of an Aberdeen express. I remember remarking on the odd spectacle it presented of GN- and GC-designed locomotives performing so blithely together on, of all places, the NB's greatest main line!

THE LMS AT GRAHAMSTON

Some of the first Dunalastairs were still spanking briskly between Larbert and Edinburgh when I was a boy. No 14319 sticks in my mind as a frequent visitor to Grahamston, if only because her maroon livery outlived that of most of her contemporaries. Pickersgill 4-4-0s were unknown at Grahamston then but soon infiltrated when Compounds arrived to share heavy main line duties through Larbert.

At least two afternoon trains a day through Grahamston were double headed, and this enabled me to witness all manner of McIntosh and Pickersgill locomotive couplings. A feature which intrigued me was the popping noise which often acted as prelude to standing starts from the station. This sound, I learned later, was only produced by superheated types amongst the Caley 4-4-0s. It came from the snifting valve, which was located on McIntosh engines and Pickersgill's first batch, low down on the side of the smokebox. Snifting valves on later Pickersgill engines were accommodated in a neat coil behind the chimney.

Another striking feature of Caledonian 4-4-0s were the massive double-bogied, eight-wheeled tenders a number of them carried. Here, I fear, my dual role got in the way; for while as a railway enthusiast I was inevitably impressed by these super-tenders, in my guise as devout NB supporter I had to admit to some vexation at the sight of a refinement to which the NB had never aspired. Still, as I used to mumble to myself—at least the Caley never had Atlantics!

THE LMS AT LARBERT

Years before I had even thought of railway photography I had made my initial acquaintance with Larbert traffic at a spot, two miles nearer Glasgow, known as Three Bridges. After making common passage with the main line out of Larbert station and across a viaduct, tracks for Falkirk and Denny respectively hived away, one on each side, in quite spectacular fashion. The resultant

61

layout looked impressive, but after a few visits one realised that all worthwhile traffic utilised the bridge in the middle, ie the main line to Glasgow Buchanan Street and the south. My friend Adam and I tholed it awhile at Three Bridges, until renewed reconnaissance by bicycle unearthed a much more delectable site, a mile or so further south, in the heart of deserted moorland. It was a spot ideally manufactured for youngsters bent on mild adventure, for, beside a signal box, an old stone footbridge offered a natural grandstand as it straddled the Caley main line. The discovery nearby of a running spring of mineral water completed our bliss. Here we could cook, eat, drink and watch trains—what more could anyone want! We christened the place 'Sour Water Well', and many were the delightful days we spent there.

Traffic heading south from Larbert did well to gather speed with maximum expedition, for not far ahead lay Cumbernauld Glen, and with it promise of much hard slogging before Cumbernauld itself, seven miles distant, was reached. The struggle commenced just past Three Bridges where triple sets of tracks were reunited just in time to rise sharply through a rocky gorge. Sitting at Sour Water Well we could hear the exhausts of the engines lengthen dramatically as, despite the momentum gained running from Larbert, they felt the impact of the gradient.

We relished in particular watching Compounds make the climb. In their beautifully maintained maroon livery and polished smokebox fittings they looked unashamedly gallant as they fought their way up the bank at the head of heavy trains. These engines really had fire in their bellies—in more ways than one! Small wonder they were such favourites with Scottish enginemen. The latter by no means abused their machines, but operating conditions throughout Scotland invoked such constant grappling with gradients and curves that locomotives which could be worked as hard as the men drove themselves were dear to the heart. Caley, NB, Highland—all had long bred engines in the same tough tradition, and the Midland Compound was hailed as a worthy successor. On the LNER the great strong Directors of 1924, to my mind, were something near the same mark—both in bark *and* bite.

Trains racing down the glen towards Larbert offered an equally diverting spectacle. Whatever their loads they were wont to dive through about 50mph, and appeared quite unconcerned by the prospect of a sweeping curve which carried them past Sour Water Well. The drivers' confidence was no doubt buttressed by the knowledge that at this point the track was suitably banked, but we, on the bridge, never failed to hold our breath as train after train tilted abruptly and swooped round the bend with engine cab and carriage roofs all but scraping the sheer rock of the ravine wall.

GROUPING AND THE CALEY

Like their NB counterparts Caledonian engines gave a spirited account of themselves in post-grouping years. So, too, did Caley men; though, as at Crewe, company employees took their own good time to accept certain LMS standard practices. The loss of Royal Blue was, understandably, a source of bitter chagrin, and to Caley men their locomotives, even clad in pristine Midland red, were never the same again. Again like Crewe, St Rollox men rebelled against the enforced provision of Midland-type smokebox number plates. Most Caley locos so fitted when they visited workshops early in the amalgamation managed somehow to 'lose' their plates by the time a subsequent visit was required. I observe that even in the mid-1930s one or two of the larger McIntosh 4-4-0s carried rebellion a shade further by sporting their small circular shed code plates well up in the top half of their smokeboxes.

Conversely, Caley men clung to practices of their own. Oil lamps mounted high on cab sidesheets had been a Caley hallmark for decades. Company men saw no reason why the habit should perish, and goods engines in particular observed the custom right up to the war years. Caley bufferbeam semaphore codes did not, however, receive the same tolerance. The small white twin-armed semaphores vanished rapidly from main line trains, and by the early 1930s, as far as Larbert was concerned, only trains running to and from Edinburgh were to be seen bearing them. One can only presume running staffs at Dalry Road and Stirling had 100

63

per cent proof Caley blood in their veins, for they stubbornly observed the ritual right up to 1939.

CALEDONIAN 4-6-0s

Although the Caley brought eighty-five 4-6-0s, of ten different classes, to LMS books in 1923, these locos did not survive post-grouping years as gamely as the much larger classes of 4-4-0. By the end of 1936, though Pickersgill's classes 60 and 191 were still intact, the Caley's remaining 4-6-0s, of McIntosh origin, had shrunk to a sorry figure of five.

My own favourite Caley 4-6-0s were the class 60s. Fine strapping machines, six emerged in 1916, and the LMS added twenty more, slightly modified, in 1925–6. At Larbert we saw them mainly on fish trains. To me they seemed so fleet and right as they streamed along at the head of perishable traffic. My appreciation of their sleek handsome lines was such it was as well the true facts concerning them remained a closed book to me over the years. They were, it transpired, poor performers, and their infrequent appearance on express passenger traffic was really a reflection of their inability to sustain steam and climb satisfactorily. In short, their front end was highly suspect.

Pickersgill's last 4-6-0 design was very familiar to Larbert observers. The 191s, built by NB Loco Co in 1922, were designed to meet the climb, sprint and climb again demands imposed by the vagaries of the Oban line. I am sure I never saw a tidier 4-6-0. They were dapper little engines, with 5ft 6in drivers and neatly accommodated Walschaerts valve gear. No matter at what camera angle one captured them their tidiness never deserted them, and any frontal view offered an object lesson in perspective. In keeping with the traditions of the Oban line, whose turntable facilities were cramped, the length of the 191s' tender had been kept within severe limits. They had succeeded McIntosh class 55s on Oban duties, and all eight were thus employed.

In 1935 Clan 4-6-0s were imported to share in Oban line duties. Seeing Highland locomotives work regularly through Larbert came to us as an unexpected bonus, but we insisted in regarding the 191s as the 'legitimate' Oban engines. Later the same year No 14686 *Urquhart Castle* joined the Oban ranks, but we held firm!

Latterly on the Oban line as elsewhere Stanier had the last word. From 1937 his MT 4-6-0s infiltrated with such persistence that through locomotive workings between Glasgow and Oban were adopted, and the old Caley practice of changing engines at Stirling fell by the wayside. In post-war years the Black Staniers' grip on the Oban line became absolute, and so things remained until the early 1960s when even they had to bow the knee to diesel-electric propulsion.

THE CALEY AND DOUBLE HEADING

On the main line through Larbert severe gradients, heavy loads and operating idiosyncrasies saw to it that double heading was frequently practised. During holiday periods, particularly Glasgow Fair Week, the need was even greater and the oddest of locomotive combinations were likely to be seen. The Caley hung on grimly to their share of the traffic and even while standard LMS types were swelling the ranks rapidly through the mid-1930s one still found a Caledonian locomotive involved whenever double heading through Larbert was called for.

I can recall only one exception to this rule: one Sunday morning in July 1935, when an Aberdeen-bound express entered Larbert with two Compounds, Nos 922 and 939, in front. Delighted though I was to witness this rarest of sights I could not but reflect that such an impressive conjunction of motive power seemed extravagant for a load of eight coaches!

At the other end of the scale the most bizarre coupling I contrived to record was that of 2808, a Horwich 2-6-0, piloted by 17466, a small Caley Drummond 0-6-0, as they sailed through Larbert the same week, again heading for Aberdeen—this time with *six* coaches in tow!

I was not deceived, however. There was nothing lightweight about Caley Drummond 0-6-0s, as another of them took pains to remind me later that summer. One busy Saturday afternoon a heavy train, off Stirling, drew into Larbert behind 17412 of the ilk, piloted by 14769 *Clan Cameron*, and, to my astonishment, after ditching the *Clan* the Jumbo calmly proceeded south on her own, with eleven massive coaches, including a Pullman, behind her. I obtained her picture as she left that day, but I would rather have caught her assaulting Cumbernauld Bank!

THE MCINTOSH 55

It was no doubt the vexing absence of McIntosh 4-6-0s that prompted Adam and I, more in sorrow than in hope, to visit Stirling shed one Saturday in July 1936. First to greet us, symbolic of the new order, was Stanier MT No 5008. Very charming, but not quite what we had come looking for. Hughes 2-6-0 No 2801 also lurked nearby. Never capable of resisting these most handsome of locomotives I photographed her, and as I did so a Caley 191, 14620, looking as trim as ever, wandered on to the scene.

Minutes later as the shed itself came into sight our hearts nearly burst with excitement—for there, shining in the sun, stood 14604. At long last, a class 55, McIntosh's first 4-6-0 design! She must still be working between Stirling and Oban, Adam and I reckoned darkly, for she certainly never came near Larbert. Out came our cameras, and as the 55's fireman, seeing this, obligingly moved out into open space, a sister engine, No 14605, was revealed behind, lying halfway inside the shed itself. What a day! And what luck—for by December 1936 No 14604 had been withdrawn.

Another picture that day which yielded great satisfaction was one of 14332. Only a Caley Dunalastair 11 4-4-0, but she looked so jaunty sitting there, with Pickersgill chimney fitted, and high dome, square as a Churchill hat. Sometime later, when we had completed our shed inspection, one final display of vigour came our way when 6113 *Cameronian*, her great regimental badge gleaming in the sun, thundered past on the main line, urging a fish train south with minimum delay. As Adam and I cheerfully agreed, our visit to the local Caledonian scene could not have culminated in a more noble vision.

6

Visit to Carlisle—1929

T H E morning we were due to leave for Carlisle I was awake by
the crack of dawn. I rose early with my father who, observing his
usual custom when journeying abroad, proceeded to attire himself
in best suit, raincoat and large, square bowler hat. Dressed thus,
and carrying a suitcase he had treasured for years, he looked to
my eyes a most impressive traveller. He was also a stickler for
punctuality, and well ahead of train schedule my brother and I
were marched off. My father was never the most communicative
of men when it came to divulging plans and it was only then we
learned, somewhat to our surprise, that we were travelling Caledonian to Edinburgh on this occasion. A little defensively, I
thought, he assured us his main purpose in this strategy lay in
permitting time for a walk along Princes Street gardens.

We arrived at Grahamston with ample time to spare, only to
learn our train was late. Poor father, this was one occasion where
even the certain knowledge that the Caley was the transgressor
seemed to offer little solace to his natural railwayman's chagrin.
Train time arrived and found us still watching keenly along the
½-mile straight which led in from Larbert. At last a flurry of
smoke appeared on the horizon.

The McIntosh 4-4-0 set a good example by sweeping in to a
smart stop. Her five or six coaches had hardly ceased to shudder
before father had all three of us on board. There was a hoot from
the Caley, and with a no-nonsense jerk we were off, five minutes
late by the station clock. The manner in which we accelerated
from Grahamston left little doubt as to how the train crew viewed

67

their Larbert 'connection'. We had hardly proceeded a mile when father lowered his newspaper and carefully inclined an ear to the powerful beat of the McIntosh. 'The Caley's bowfing today!' he marvelled. 'Bowfing' was the word for it. By now we were advancing up a steep rise which led to Polmont, the train was taut against its couplings, and I should think the whole neighbourhood was aware of our progress. Sparks were falling like hailstones on the carriage roof. Still climbing we joined the main LNER line west of Polmont, and hammered on non-stop through the station. Scrupulously observing the compulsory slacks at Linlithgow and Philipstoun, the Caley recovered a spanking pace without a moment's delay. Then, on the run in to Haymarket, where the Forth bridge line joins to run parallel, she really kicked up her heels. Trouble was, in the process she fairly flew past an Aberdeen express, coasting Edinburghwards behind a Reid Atlantic, and presumably handicapped by distant signals. A shade mortified behind Caledonian windows I could only gaze silently at NB passengers opposite as they glided slowly past in the wrong direction.

Now followed a brief distant view of Haymarket shed as we veered sharply right on to LMS metals. I scanned the usual early morning parade of green Pacifics, and tried to guess which one would be taking the *Flying Scotsman*. One last dash saw us past Dalry Road and into Princes Street. Father had his watch out almost before the Caley stopped. 'She's on time', he affirmed.

With father palpably in the mood to enjoy his morning stroll, my brother and I trailed behind, babbling cheerfully and pausing when he did to admire an occasional flower-bed. It did not take long for periodic drifts of steam from the concealed railway cutting to prove a powerful distraction. Latterly, so tormented did I become, I begged leave to run on ahead; to which proposal father agreed with surprising benevolence. I guess he knew where to find us! Off we scuttled, my brother and I. First stop, Waverley bridge, for a quick look at traffic in the west end of the station. *Gladiateur*, running light, chose that moment to clank in from Haymarket in lordly fashion. Now we knew who was to haul the 'Flyer'.

By the time our party reassembled the *Thames–Forth* express awaited our pleasure. At the ticket barrier, as LNER passengers, we were directed to the rear of the train. NB stock, I noted wanly, and paused to eye the superior upholstery of the M & NB Joint Stock coaches lying further down the platform. The gesture was not lost on my father. For a moment as I fixed upon him an expression compounded equally of hope and innocence his NB conscience positively wavered. With some effort loyalty prevailed. 'Our ticket is NB', he gruffed. Dutifully I lumped our luggage aboard one of the rear coaches.

Now, with seats earmarked we were at liberty to watch for our engine arriving. Down we went, past the lovely crimson clerestory-roofed Midland stock, just in time to witness a remarkable sight as, midst clouds of smoke and steam, a train burst forth from the portals of Calton tunnel. At its head, coupled to an N2 0-6-2 tank, a Director, *Malcolm Graeme*, ran tender first. Both engines were barking and belching so furiously we were thoroughly deceived—until eighteen coaches sailed past, to reveal another N2 pushing hard at the rear. It was empty stock coming up from Leith. An exciting prelude to the morning, but one promptly put behind us when a large green tender emerged from the tunnel mouth and proceeded to bear down steadily upon us. Our own train engine had arrived from St Margarets. We jostled excitedly to catch the Atlantic's number as she weaved in. My brother was first. '9906!' he called out. '*Teribus!*' I cried.

Teribus it was. She looked magnificent, green and polished and purposeful, and proudly we laid claim to her as the fireman coupled up. On top of her massive smokebox she carried the familiar curved NB destination board. On her buffer beam sat two of the whitest train lamps I have ever seen.

With the *Thames–Forth* locomotive now in position the railway temperature at Waverley east rose appreciably. Indeed, a heartwarming spectacle was rapidly falling into place about us. Away to our left an immaculate *Gladiateur* now simmered gracefully at the head of the *Flying Scotsman*, while her driver fussed at a cylinder before an admiring audience. Another lithe green Pacific approached on our right to complete the panorama by backing quietly on to the *Scotsman*'s running partner, the 10.15 for King's Cross. It was *Neil Gow*. Spectators began to cluster in turn about her. Suddenly, as if determined not to be outshone by such distinguished company, *Teribus* took a hand in the game. There was a crack like cannon shot, and glorious triple sheafs of white steam cascaded from her safety valves. She was as ready for the road as any Pacific!

Shortly before ten my father, professing to be a little anxious lest we should fail to board our train, joined us. Having calculated he was unlikely to resist seeing the 'Flyer' off, we were not surprised. Another inspection of *Teribus* was carried out under his aegis, and the steam coach *Flower of Yarrow* trundled in from points east to add her green and cream to an already colourful scene. The huge clock above the station moved inexorably towards the hour, and exactly on ten an excited chain reaction of whistles from No 1 platform reached our ears. The *Flying Scotsman*'s time had come.

The southbound start from Waverley is unspectacular and lends itself to a minimum of locomotive fuss. In response to promptings, from everywhere except the footplate it seemed, *Gladiateur*'s sleek chimney emitted the merest wisp of steam, her driving wheels, glistening in the sun, lazily summed up the situation, and she moved gently off. Father quickly resumed command and as we were dispatched to our seats I looked back in time to see the last of the 'Flyer's' long train of shapely East Coast stock snake out towards Calton tunnel. A few moments later, at 10.3 precisely, *Teribus* followed in her wake. Our long awaited trip to Carlisle was under way.

The journey east from Edinburgh through city environs is a dignified affair of momentum gently gathered. No apparent exertion, no fireworks, but an essentially genteel procedure singularly reminiscent of life in the capital itself. The thought has often occurred to me that this calm exodus from Waverley, compared to the uninhibited storming scramble from Glasgow Queen Street, offered more than a superficial guide to life itself in the two great cities. *Teribus*, albeit a product of Glasgow, behaved herself that fine morning.

page 71
LMS No 14639, one of the post-grouping Caledonian '60' class, passing Larbert with a fish train in July 1935

Scotland's only Moguls. (*above*) Peter Drummond's G & SW 2-6-0
of 1915 as LMS No 17830 makes a rare appearance on a passenger
train at Glasgow (St Enoch) in August 1936; (*below*) LMS No 17804
(ex-CR No 38) at Perth in August 1936

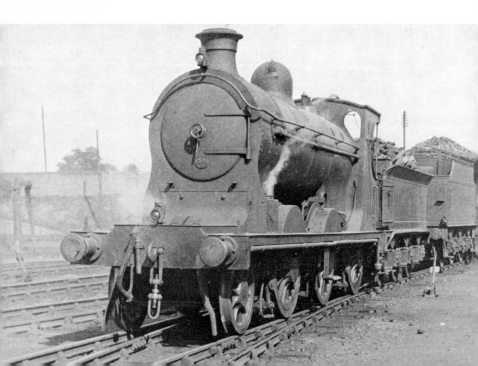

THE WAVERLEY ROUTE

Soon I discovered why my father regarded the 'road to Carlisle' with such respect. Trains bound for Berwick have a warming gallop across East Lothian to their credit before Cockburnspath presents itself. Carlisle trains were less fortunate. Their engines had to be in good trim from the word 'go', for immediately after the short gentle drop into Portobello East the Waverley line hardened without ceremony into a 1 in 80 gradient to Niddrie East. Thus soon the gloves were off, and for the next 13 miles sheer grinding work faced any southbound locomotive.

It was thrilling to hear *Teribus* get down to her task. Her previously easy-going exhaust sharpened, until latterly the hillsides rang with her bark as Falahill took its toll. Station names I had heard of, but never seen—Newtongrange, Gorebridge, Fushiebridge—began to slide past, and prompted me to stick my head from the window. *Teribus,* looking a picture, toiled on ahead, her coupling rods flashing in the sun; but I barely had time to focus half-closed eyes on her lovely green bulk before the barrage of sparks she was putting up drove me back inside. I retired to the corridor, whence my father, seeing me impressed by my new surroundings, joined me. It gave him an opportunity of advancing my railway education by pointing out check rails and catch points, and explaining their purpose.

By the time *Teribus* had blasted her way to the summit father and I were deep in mutual contemplation of the plight of a goods guard making a similar trip—only, this time in pitch darkness, and with No 186 performing at the head. Even at my tender age I had seen the inside of a guard's van and found no difficulty in picturing the eerie scene—the oil lamp swinging overhead, the coal stove glowing steadily, the hard brutal edges of woodwork as the van bumped and swayed and snatched, entirely at the dictate of the load in front. Imagine coming to a full stop on Falahill, then bracing yourself for the awful grab as the clash of couplings rings down the restarted train and creeps nearer and nearer until finally, with complete caprice, you are hurled once more on into darkness. Yet this man loved his job.

Down we went, past Fountainhall and Bowland, free now from

the burden of Falahill, yet unable, because of the tortuous nature of the route, to take full advantage of our change of fortune. How different things would have been on Cockburnspath!

Soon we drew into Galashiels's island platform. 'Shed on the left', murmured my father, reading my thoughts aright. Outside the shed *Rob Roy*, first of the unsuperheated Scotts, stood cheek by jowl with a class C 0-6-0. Further round the side a 0-6-0 superheater dozed and looked sleek in the sun. *Teribus* eased her train away confidently, and ahead of us, along the foot of the Eildon hills, stretched a lush fertile valley. Not far beyond lay Melrose, with its ruined abbey, and St Boswells, separated only by the river from Dryburgh abbey, last resting place of two great men of Scotland, Sir Walter Scott and Earl Haig. My father was now completely in his element. Gently and proudly he revealed his intimate knowledge of the beautiful countryside. I noticed that a sight of the Tweed in particular seemed to move him deeply.

By far the least strenuous section of the Waverley route was the central part. Even then the line rose and fell continuously over the 19 miles which separated Galashiels and Hawick. Stops at Melrose and St Boswells placed a doubly effective premium on cross-country sprinting. One ex-NE 4-4-0 reposed at St Boswells's small shed, no doubt waiting to work back on the Duns line once the *Thames–Forth* had gone.

The shed at Hawick was larger, with every locomotive in sight NB in origin. The station itself was built on a high embankment overlooking the town, but I failed to appreciate the vicious standing start it presented to trains bound for Carlisle. *Teribus* was taking water, and I was watching her when my father spoke.

'Are we taking on a pilot?' he enquired. I looked back down the line and was astonished to find we were. A class C 0-6-0 was quietly approaching the rear of our train. Amused by my look of surprise my father invited me to read the gradient board which stood at the end of the platform. It read 1 in 75. Apart from that, he went on to explain, we were standing right now on the first of a series of severe reverse curves, and for the next 10 miles or so *Teribus* would really have her work cut out climbing Whitrope summit. Falahill, it appeared, was only an aperitif.

He was right, as usual. None of us could resist watching the start from the open window. A wild exchange of cockcrows rang out and *Teribus* got off to a powerful start; thanks to our old friend, the C, for we could feel the assistance from behind. Once clear of the platform the pilot dropped back, and singlehanded the long tough haul got under way. Occasional glimpses of the town proffered themselves as we wound up and away from Hawick, until, finally, the surrounding hills closed in. Directly ahead the terrain looked bleak.

Stobs, 4 miles out, appeared from nowhere. I looked round the desolate landscape, added mentally the rigours of winter, and shuddered. Four miles more and we were through Shankend, faced now with the last, and worst, stretch of the climb. Out front we could hear *Teribus* roaring as never before. Then, at father's abrupt command, windows were closed. Whitrope tunnel was imminent.

Whistle screaming, *Teribus* was really shooting out sparks as we plunged into darkness, and the curtain of fire which streaked past our windows, coupled with the din from the Atlantic as she made her supreme effort, combined, I remember, to create such an unreal world that the act of re-emerging into daylight proved a distinct shock. Smoke cleared. We were *still* climbing! Father, as excited by now as his two sons, huddled us round the window to watch for the summit at Whitrope box. I wonder if the signalman noticed three people that morning gesticulating like dervishes as the *Thames–Forth* breasted the climb and disposed of the last serious barrier between herself and England?

No less frustrating to an engine driver than the descent from Falahill was the south side of Whitrope, with its drop through Liddesdale. Again chronic curvature offset the advantage offered by gravity and the locomotive had to be kept severely in check. In this respect the Waverley route was remarkable enough amongst the country's main lines, but as a wide desolate valley opened up ahead an even more remarkable phenomenon was about to materialise before my eyes. For the station which lay ahead was Riccarton Junction; and Riccarton, my father assured us solemnly, had positively no access by road. It was, in the literal sense, a 'railway village'.

With the magic of 13 miles intervening Hawick now assumed the role of metropolis. Stores came from there to Riccarton by rail, children journeyed to school by train, either to Hawick or Newcastleton—as did churchgoers (free of charge!) on Sundays—while, once or twice a week, a special late train from Hawick enabled local residents to sample the erotic delights of an evening at the cinema. The refreshment room, too, on Riccarton's island platform obviously served higher purpose, judging by the number of citizens who waved the *Thames–Forth* on her way! This was not the first time I had observed friendliness along the line, but it was here I realised most graphically that on a route such as the Waverley the passing of trains must be daily events of some consequence.

Once the wild valley at Riccarton was crossed, and we were through Steele Road, the landscape about us mellowed appreciably, until by Newcastleton an aspect much akin to that of the true Scott country again presented itself. Father reminded us we were passing through what used to be great feuding country—like so many of his generation he was thoroughly versed in the Waverley novels—and we were remarshalled close to the window so that nothing should be missed of a promised sequence of events. First instructions were to watch out for a large house appearing on the horizon. All three of us peered out as if our lives depended on it. Father fidgeted, then—'There!' he exclaimed dramatically, and pointed through what was, to me at least, impenetrable foliage by the lineside.

I looked, happened to catch my brother's eye in the process—and knew he had seen nothing either. There seemed no point in spoiling father's pleasure, so we both nodded dutifully. Father leaned back, and assumed the look of one who reminisces. 'There was racing and chasing on Cannibalee', he intoned; an observation which puzzled me mightily at the time. This odd procedure was to persist on subsequent trips we made to Carlisle, and never failed to baffle me. Then one year I saw the light, and things fell into place. The word was, of course, 'Canobie Lea'.

Next on the agenda was the Border, by now less than 3 miles distant. Came the warning, and inspired by memories of similar acts of homage near Berwick my brother and I braced ourselves for the Grand Salute. Hard by Kershopefoot station a small burn trickled beneath us. My father relaxed. 'That's it', he announced. This time I swear there was a distinct twinkle in his eye.

Twenty more miles to Carlisle. By the time we reached Riddings Junction the surrounding countryside had flattened, and the Rivers Esk and Liddel wound devious patterns by our side. Longtown, Lyneside, Harker. For a brief spell *Teribus* revelled in unaccustomed luxury, that of a straight level road, and rapidly increasing proximity to Carlisle began to generate its own excitement. Father bade us watch for the Caley main line pass below, and was additionally rewarded by extreme agitation on my part as the Caley at Kingmoor came into sight. The shed was full, and the view a panoramic one; but, oh, so tantalisingly distant that as we swung away I was reduced to identifying familiar shapes. What a harvest might have been reaped! One final stab of frustration struck home as something massive and crimson moved slowly along behind smoking ranks, and caught my eye in the bright sunshine. The Silloth line joined us, and tension mounted as the NB approach to Carlisle prepared to sweep round towards the city in two great opposing curves.

CARLISLE CITADEL

As our train entered Citadel station the first locomotive I saw, a large tank in the act of moving out, had me guessing. The purely fleeting glimpse I obtained revealed leading six-coupled driving wheels, and from the length of her I knew a trailing bogie must follow. All else I could tell was that she was built along substantial lines and bore a five-digit number, commencing 169--. That meant she was Scottish. Or did it? I wondered, recalling a little uneasily Horwich 2-6-0s and Fowler dock tanks I had seen bearing 'Scottish' numbers of a sort. Yet I was sure the tank was not Caledonian. All very vexing. Meanwhile, the *Thames–Forth* drew to a halt on Carlisle's Main Up platform, and persuaded me to shelve the problem in favour of more immediate excitements. Later that afternoon time for reflection reminded me that locomotives of a third Scottish company besides the NB and

Caledonian were valid visitors to Carlisle. The mystery tank was, of course, a Glasgow & South Western 0-6-2.

Citadel station impressed me the moment I set foot on the platform. Not that the process took long; I was out before *Teribus* could draw breath, to find the arrival of the *Thames–Forth* had released all the buzz of excitement which so pervades great railway stations, and I wasted no time in getting down to the engine. The fireman was already down below uncoupling *Teribus*. Presently the driver eased back to permit the link coupling to be disconnected, and within a minute of my arrival the Reid Atlantic ambled off. What on earth would the Midland provide in lieu?

I was engrossed in peering from the station in what I deemed to be a Midland direction when the rest of my family arrived. 'Here comes the Midland', I heard my father say, whereupon I abandoned my empty horizon and turned to behold a brace of 4-4-0s slipping out from cover of our own coaches. There was a sight, if you please. My first Midland engines! Hardly in gleaming Derby red, though, as I had dreamed—for each was as black as the ace of spades. The two locos coasted forward, bringing with them extra coaches to compensate for NB stock since detached at the rear.

A closer look as they threaded back into the main platform verified that both were vintage Midland in design. There was no mistaking that superbly tidy amalgam of line and curve. There, too, were all the hallmarks: the Belpaire firebox, the snugly saddled smokebox, the slender capuchoned chimney, the elegant sweep of the cab roof. Even the brass numerals mounted high on each cabside impressed me. Trust the Midland to think up a stylish way of displaying even a locomotive's power rating. Just then *Teribus* passed back, running light through the station. I was surprised to observe how sophisticated she now looked in her matchless green livery, when viewed in the context of two rugged black Midland 4-4-0s.

With departure imminent both engines were blowing hard and seemed raring to go. There is a thrill about watching a double-headed train which increases to an acute degree when the

78

coupled power of the engines is transformed into movement. The Midland locomotives did not disappoint me. At the first shrill of the guard's whistle both crews were ready for action; those on the train engine possibly over-ready—for, while both machines took shrewd deep initial blasts, the class 3 almost immediately contrived to over-reach herself. Her coupling rods span into a blur, the engine herself shook violently, and a great column of smoke shot high into Citadel's vaulted roof, while, beneath my feet, the platform trembled and I feared a little, though thoroughly relishing the pyrotechnics.

The class 2 pilot, left to cope, took the strain, and as we watched slowly dragged the load—class 3, coaches and all. It was magnificent, but fortunately perhaps for the smaller engine her erring partner's paroxysm proved to be of brief duration. Recovering her composure the class 3 started afresh, and soon added a crisp beat to the syncopation with which the gallant pair bade adieu to Carlisle. Longing to be aboard I watched the *Thames–Forth* as she wound her way out and off to foreign parts. She had disappeared from sight and I was still gazing south when my father appeared at my elbow to remind me gently that lunch was indicated.

Lunch was mercifully brief. On our way back I remember plodding ahead of the main party towards railway lines which crossed the foot of a park, when the sight of a strange black object sailing slowly past 50yd distant fairly electrified me. My first LNW engine! The 0-8-0 offered a vivid contrast to anything I had previously known, and lean lines and uncompromising black livery bestowed on her a look of austerity even the Caley could not approach. Yet there was a majesty about this machine.

With excitement mounting so rapidly it was as well Citadel lay not far away. Father settled himself comfortably on a station bench and, at last, my brother and I were free to roam. We were crossing the footbridge which led to the central platform when I spotted a very large engine standing light at the London end of the station. The excitement which whooped within me as I raced forward to investigate remains with me to this day.

I am not likely to forget my first sight of a Royal Scot. *Planet* faced south and stood tender first as I approached, offering an aspect which even accentuated the girth of her massive boiler, and underlined the fact that her great square firebox *tilted back* to join the cab. My eyes, accustomed to size and grace *vide* Gresley's Pacifics, opened wide, I am sure, in astonishment. In the half light of Citadel station her rich maroon livery and gold lettering positively glowed.

The abiding impression this engine conveyed was one of power. Unlike Gresley's creations, with their gently tapering front ends, *Planet*'s great barrelled boiler thrust forward uncompromising as a ramrod, and terminated bluntly only just short of the buffer beam. I had never imagined, much less seen, a boiler of this size before, nor had I deemed a chimney could be so minute. The Belpaire firebox so closely approached maximum permissible dimensions it had been inclined to permit the installation of safety valve and (horizontal) whistle. Below the running-plate cylinders, motion and wheel assembly were compatible with Gresley's. The wheelbase was equally tight and elegant, yet in the case of the Royal Scot one had a distinct feeling that the upper works were overmassive, and were bound to crush the frail mechanism below. Beneath *Planet*'s brief nameplate the LMS had mounted their master touch, an oval brass plaque bearing the etched outline of an ancient locomotive which had once borne the name. The cab appeared to be a businesslike development of Midland practice, while the tender, neatly shaped in Fowler fashion, was only precluded from appearing too small by the accident of being heaped high with coal.

Planet was obviously waiting to take over a south-bound express. I might have gaped long enough had not a small black object, backing in towards the Maryport bay, caught my eye. I guessed it was a Jumbo, but was hardly prepared to find even a 2-4-0 quite so toylike. Still, her minute dimensions, coupled with the discovery that her name was *Bee* (shades of *Vich Ian Vohr!*), did something towards repairing the dent caused to my LNER morale by the superb appearance of *Planet*. *Bee*'s thin curved nameplate, with its sunken black-waxed lettering, I rather liked, as I did the bare functional look of the engine. I found it hard, though, to swallow that microscopic machines like this had performed valorous deeds on Shap. Further reflections on the subject, however, were cut short as a second Royal Scot rolled in at the head of the awaited London express.

Ah, this time a military name—*Royal Inniskilling Fusilier*— and how lovely she looked! *Planet* eased forward and for a few moments the two massive crimson locomotives shone together in all their glory. A North Eastern 4-4-0, her great brass-beaded double splasher answering defiantly for the LNER, backed in on to a Newcastle train, and I remember standing there in complete awe as the southern end of Citadel station revealed its delights. Within ten minutes all three trains had gone, and I took advantage of the temporary lull to report first impressions back to my father. He listened, and appeared pleased at my excitement. Had I seen a Claughton yet? No, I hadn't. 'You will', he assured me, and resumed his newspaper.

It was silly of me to have doubted the Jumbos' prowess. Ten minutes later an unlikely-looking combination appeared on the high approach from Crewe. The long train was double headed, and presently the odd pair defined themselves as a Jumbo and Claughton respectively.

How strange it was. The Premier Line never had time or patience for such refinements as flush-headed rivets, they painted their locos jet black, every other aspect of their locomotive construction was unashamedly austere and functional—yet express engines born of Crewe thrust at one an air of unmistakable authority. Even as I watched the new arrivals bustle in, the spell of the LNW laid its hands on me, and the possibility of these same two characters raising hell on Shap summit suddenly seemed very real.

To be true, the LMS had imposed maroon livery on this, my first, Claughton, *Private E. Sykes VC*. I could sense it sat uneasily on her, but I thought her a noble sight just the same. Her calm dignified demeanour seemed almost to protect the tiny Jumbo who fussed so earnestly in front, for although *Thomas Carlyle*'s driving wheels were no smaller than those of her companion, her coupling rods somehow conveyed every impression of revolving twice as busily. Later, when the two locomotives passed back, running light for the North Western shed, I was intrigued to note that nothing had changed. *Private Sykes* coasted elegantly and the Jumbo retained still the pained expression of one who was doing all the work.

Within the hour my LNW education proceeded apace, when a Prince drifted on to the scene and positioned herself by the southern end of the station. I gaped at her for some time, impressed by her size and rawness, baffled by her absence of name; for I had no way of knowing quite a few of these 4-6-0s were nameless. The slight depression this discovery induced in me was easily dispelled when a Precursor laboured in from the south, her thin nameplate gleaming in the sun. Good heavens—*Thunderbolt!* This bravura style of naming the LNW affected was beginning to excite me. Soon after, such is life, the arrival on the scene of an equally exotic name nearly proved my undoing. I had just made one of my periodic reports back to my father, when my brother spoke.

'Surely,' he observed, 'that was a Precursor came in just now?'

'It was', I riposted happily. '5219—*Fish.*'

'Who?'

'*Fish!*'

My brother thought for a few seconds. 'How do you spell it?' he enquired warily. Confidently, out came my notebook. 'P-s-y-c-h-e', I announced; and, as I reached the 'e', recalled, too late, my brother had studied Greek at school. There was silence for a moment.

'I think', said he, speaking from a great height, 'you mean "Si-ky" '. 'I think', said I, responding desperately from a greater height, 'it counts just the same'—and dashed off to catch *Fish* second time round.

All too quickly the few hours at our disposal drifted past, and late afternoon found the three of us reunited at the northern end of the station, gazing with unconcealed awe at *Liddesdale* as she stood on a central road, three or four NB coaches behind her, patiently awaiting her St Pancras 'connection'. Father was in good form—the Reid Atlantic looked superb; and tut-tutted good

naturedly—the Midland was late. Fifteen minutes behind schedule
two Midland 4-4-0s hoisted their train into Citadel. They looked
tired, had obviously had a rough trip, and I think all three of us
felt a little ashamed. Off came the Midland engines, back came
Liddesdale, and we were aboard.

The station staff, too, were alive to the occasion, for within
minutes the lamps of the Caley goods yard were slipping past us
in the gathering dusk. I settled down in my NB seat and listened
with deep content to *Liddesdale*'s beat. Soon, disposed to relax
and dream idly of a monumental day's railway activity, I leaned
back, and murmured to the others to be sure I missed nothing of
consequence on the way home. Next thing I knew, my elbow was
being gently shaken.

I looked up. It was my father.

'Waverley', he said. 'All change'—and grinned.

7

West to East

I n the mid-1930s a decision by railway management to fight the growing menace of bus transport saw the institution of a 1s 6d Saturday afternoon fare for the return journey from Falkirk to Glasgow. Apart from coinciding conveniently with my own decision to attend an academy in Glasgow for further violin tuition, it helped to correct in my railway habits a pronounced penchant for travelling east. The latter, of course, was the product of my father's earnest conviction that at holiday times all worthwhile railway tracks led to the Borders. So for the next two years my favourite Saturday pastime became travelling into Glasgow via Buchanan Street, and returning home from Queen Street. That way I had the best of both railway worlds.

THE LMS IN GLASGOW

For a city of its size Glasgow's four main stations were remarkably compactly grouped together. Central station was well named and lay within comfortable walking distance of the others. Its prime purpose lay in tending the Caledonian's link with the south; though, of course, it handled a good deal of ancillary traffic besides, plus a lively Cathcart Circle suburban service. The original installation at Central dated back to 1879, and had been built to relieve Buchanan Street which, from its inception thirty years earlier, had been handling all Caledonian traffic to and from the south. Later Central station was enlarged and massive engineering energy was spent in developing a new bridged approach over the River Clyde.

Buchanan Street station, only half a mile distant, had had a chequered career. Nearly as old as the Caledonian railway itself it lost much of its prestige when traffic to the south was hived off to Central. Least impressive in size and appearance of all the Glasgow stations Buchanan Street had, nevertheless, to be geared to handle abnormally heavy north-bound traffic during holiday periods, and could offer many a stirring sight of double-headed expresses charging fiercely up through St Rollox.

Odd man out in the LMS Glasgow trinity was St Enoch, Glasgow & South Western stronghold since 1876. The passage of post-amalgamation time had seen St Enoch's rumbustious rivalry with Central for west coast traffic subside into something resembling fair shares, but it was well known (or, at least, NB men were well aware!) that beneath the surface old differences still smouldered between G & SW and the Caley. Poor Caley, how they suffered in the good old days. Even Highland men viewed them with deep suspicion. The penalty, possibly, of success?

QUEEN STREET STATION

Passengerwise the NB held its own at Queen Street, the fourth of the Glasgow termini, and it was from there a citizen usually ventured if he wished to sample the more delectable aspects of life east of Glasgow. It must be confessed the NB did not offer the brightest of starts to his journey.

Queen Street station was cavernous, gloomy and glass roofed, yet built on such a comparatively subdued scale that a traveller seeing the NB's Glasgow terminal for the first time was unlikely to be spared a feeling of distinct anticlimax; particularly if he had passed through Waverley en route. Would-be passengers stepped without ado from the street into what must have seemed an underground cave, and many who did so must have been blissfully unaware that beneath their feet, even deeper in the bowels of the earth, lurked yet another Queen Street station, Low Level. A considerable volume of passenger suburban traffic passed through the latter daily but throughout the years I visited Glasgow I cannot recall ever feeling an urge to explore its murky depths.

The main station aloft suffered from severe disabilities. The passenger area behind the platform ends was cramped and easily defied description as a concourse, while the atmosphere of congestion already established was painfully underlined by the almost incessant thrashing of Westinghouse air pumps. The noise came mainly from ex-NB class A 0-6-2 tanks. Now LNER class N14, these engines graduated from Cowlairs, via the NB Locomotive Co, in 1909, and had spent their lives since banking trains up Cowlairs incline. No matter what time of day one visited Queen Street one of them was usually to be observed close up to the ramps, coupled behind its train, patiently awaiting departure, and content meanwhile to pant for dear life.

Rolling stock and motive power to be seen around the 1930s varied largely according to the train I was pursuing. If I elected to return to Falkirk via Larbert, or direct to Grahamston, I would have to settle for a train composed almost entirely of ex-NB stock. Not the most luxurious way of rounding off a Saturday afternoon, but at least the absence of corridors afforded maximum mobility once an empty compartment had been secured. Travelling thus offered one consolation: I could be certain the LNER would enhance the pre-grouping illusion by providing an NB 4-4-0 in front. If an Edinburgh express, stopping at Falkirk High or Polmont, better suited my purpose this meant boarding a train made up entirely of the LNER's familiar and quite beautiful East Coast stock, headed by, in all probability, a Director or Shire.

A couple of platforms away West Highland trains, once the proud reserve of Glens and NB Intermediates, now left Glasgow behind Lochs, while at the tunnel end of the platform an occasional 0-6-0 sidetank, ex-NB class D, now J83, might be seen lingering on station pilot duties. Built by Matthew Holmes in 1900 these little tanks pioneered rear-banking duties at the turn of the century when the famous Cowlairs cable haulage was abandoned. They clung to the task until Reid's 0-6-2 tanks took over in 1909.

COWLAIRS TUNNEL

The east end of the station conveyed even more vividly the gloomy nature of the Queen Street environment. The lines from three island platforms converged sharply to pass under a wide, crowded signal gantry which was in turn straddled by a high, latticed road bridge. Thence the tracks funnelled into a sheer-sided stone-faced ravine, where a profusion of coloured advertisement-bearing enamelled plates grappled vainly with a soot-laden atmosphere. Entry into Cowlairs tunnel itself was achieved in such short space of time that a departing locomotive and its leading coach were absorbed into its grim depths before the last coach had left the platform.

Departure reeked of noise and energy. At the appropriate whistle from the train engine the tank at the rear would utter a sharp shriek and set immediately to work. One felt the buffet from behind as it lent its strength towards lifting the heavy train. Track within the station was almost level, but no sooner had it entered the tunnel than the vicious gradient of 1 in 45 made its presence felt. A decent start was therefore imperative.

Carriage windows left open had soon hurriedly to be closed, for the briefest intrusion into the tunnel produced volumes of dense sulphurous fumes, and the earnest beat of two engines, bouncing from the tunnel walls, soon magnified within a compartment into a thunderous roar. Cowlairs tunnel was only 1,000yd long but the act of traversing it always seemed to me an eternity. In an effort to relieve the tedium I used to count the air shafts as their stabs of daylight filtered slowly past, and watch the thick rolls of smoke yellow again as the weaker illumination from within the coach regained command.

Evidence of the third and last shaft was always welcome. Even then the maelstrom of smoke and grit which accompanied our exit from the tunnel remained so impenetrable to the eye for some time that, but for the sudden key change in acoustics, there was little evidence we were once again in the open. Presently the fog cleared and train engine and pilot struggled on up the bank. At the top as one's coach slowly entered Cowlairs station a glance back revealed the true nature of the incline. Seen even from the height of a moving train the permanent way stretched back, then simply disappeared. From a Glasgow-bound driver's point of view the drop must have seemed positively frightening, even with train brakes firmly applied.

87

Now, too, was the time to watch the rear of the train as, on reaching the summit, the pilot tank slipped her couplings. The train, suddenly on level ground, would quicken visibly and the gap between ourselves and pilot widen as the latter, now coasting, followed up through the station, her task complete. By then the gaunt shapes of foundries and erecting shops at Cowlairs locomotive works, obtruding on my left, demanded my attention.

At Cowlairs railway casualties awaiting treatment stretched outside in the yard in two long lines and were clearly visible from passing trains. Mostly they were ex-NB locomotives. Occasionally a Director would show up, or a Darlington-sired J39 or Shire, but I cannot recollect seeing a Doncaster-built engine in any of the processions—and certainly never a Gresley Pacific. Doncaster, it seemed, like the devil, looked after its own! The lifeless locos on display, often tenderless, sometimes partly dismantled, always looked weathered and careworn, but at worst they were innocent of the doom-laden air that was to hallmark similar queues fifteen years later.

Almost immediately Eastfield running shed was due on the right, and this, too, was not to be missed. The NB's two largest sheds, like their cities, presented vastly different public faces, but there was no doubt that Edinburgh, in the form of Haymarket, with its cohorts of gleaming green, silver and blue Pacifics, had the edge over Eastfield. Poor Eastfield, charged with supplying motive power to a variety of routes less dashing than the East Coast and Aberdeen main lines, played a comparatively plebian role. Still, any depot with fourteen running roads and a full house of 100 locos was worth watching, and I kept a close eye on Eastfield.

Next attraction was the marshalling yards at Cadder. These were extensive and bounded both sides of the tracks. My father spoke so much of Cadder I could never resist especial scrutiny of goods vans amongst the freight trains inevitably to be seen working there. Many times I waved to guards, but none of them proved to be the one I was looking for!

After Cadder, Lenzie Junction, where a branch line diving off down through Back o' Loch Halt held memories. When I was

LMS No 17929 (ex-Highland Railway 'Jones goods' built by Sharp Stewart & Co Ltd in 1894) at Perth in August 1934

page 90
Express Jumbos. (*above*) LMS No 17412 (CR Jumbo No 745 built
in 1895) leaving Larbert for Glasgow (Buchanan St) with an enormous
Pullman car express in July 1935; (*below*) LMS No 17466 (CR Jumbo
No 763 built in 1896) displays express passenger headlamps as it
pilots LMS 2-6-0 No 2808 on a Glasgow–Aberdeen train in July 1935

very young I used to spend holidays with an aunt there, and in these days LNER suburban trains from Glasgow frequently consisted of twin sets of Gresley's triple-articulated coaches. Even motive power was supplied by Gresley, in the shape of his powerful N2 0-6-2 tanks. Just like King's Cross, had I but known! Back o' Loch Halt was on a stiff gradient between Lenzie and Kirkintilloch, but the N2s were delightfully sure-footed creatures.

From Lenzie onwards trains bound for Edinburgh could settle down to a fair gallop along straight, level terrain. Croy, Dullatur, Castlecary—then just before Bonnybridge the Caley main line from Buchanan Street passed underneath. Greenhill marshalling yards marked the spot where the two main lines established the link which benefited NB purposes. Soon Falkirk's industrial environment began to assert itself, and our LNER train was sailing through familiar and well-loved territory. Immediately beyond Falkirk High station a tunnel lay in wait. Once this was breached two miles of exhilarating speed was feasible before the approach of Polmont Junction saw brakes firmly applied. This was my cue to rise, change trains and return to Falkirk by humbler means.

POLMONT STATION

Polmont to me will always mean holiday trips to the Borders, for a very necessary prelude was our trundling up from Grahamston by branch train. At Polmont, whichever NB tank pulled our train up could rely on her reward varying little at the end of it all. She would be given about two minutes flat to discharge passengers, pull out from the station, and set her two-coach train back into the Bo'ness bay, or 'dock', as NB men styled it.

Waiting at Polmont to change trains was never a hardship. My keen sense of anticipation that our journey east from Waverley lay less than an hour distant was heightened by the act of waiting to see which type of engine would loom round the bend at the head of our Edinburgh express. Pacifics and Shires I could have identified with my eyes shut because of their clanking approach, Scotts had a habit of bustling in briskly, Directors entered with greater aplomb, while the sight of an NB Atlantic sailing into

Polmont at the head of an Edinburgh express had a majesty that made the spirits soar.

There was, too, the electric undercurrent of a passenger-crowded platform, and porters stood alertly by luggage and parcels piled at carefully adjudged spots along the platform. The station foreman, a familiar figure whose uniform indicated superior status, added to my secret boyish pride when, as often as not, my father and he would while away time by engaging publicly in conversation. Once the incoming train was sighted the foreman went off down the platform to supervise loading—and share in the train announcement, for public-address equipment for the purpose did not exist in those days.

Looking back, though, the really evocative element amongst the sounds of an East Coast express rolling into Polmont station comes to me down the years by courtesy of an Irish porter, a non-descript little character who wandered about the station, bearing a cheerful grin which never left him. He had in addition a voice of pure silver, and as the arrival of the express kindled a stirring along the crowded platform the little Irishman would bustle along its length, his voice soaring high and clear above the hubbub. 'Polmont', he would sing, 'Edinburgh Waverley–King's Cross train'. It sounded like a litany.

MANUEL AND BO'NESS

Next station east of Polmont owed its existence to the fact that alone it offered an outlet for rail traffic to and from Bo'ness docks—Manuel (the very name implied seafaring history). It was one of several Portuguese-sounding names which cropped up around the Forth estuary. Nearer Edinburgh one came across Ratho, and east of the city Portobello and Joppa added their quota of romantic history. Here at Manuel a single track which clambered up from Bo'ness diverged, one prong forking right to join the main line, while the other passed on through Manuel Low Level station underneath, and, still climbing, went on towards Slamannan and Bathgate.

Having heard my father speak fulsomely of rail traffic handled at Bo'ness during World War I, I expected to find there an NB dock installation almost analagous to the Caledonian network at Grangemouth, but when I first visited Bo'ness in 1934 I was chagrined to find them very small indeed. Worse still, one solitary J88 0-6-0 tank appeared to be dealing quite comfortably, thank you, with all shunting requirements! Still, No 9289 was a distinctive little engine in her own rights, for her class emerged in 1905 as W. P. Reid's first contribution to NB motive power. 9289's tall chimney and dumb wooden buffers may have given her an old-fashioned look, but her extremely short wheelbase suited her needs when it came to worming her way round the tight curves and neglected metals of Bo'ness docks.

Railwaywise Bo'ness had a weary look. The passenger station, a mere single platform, looked as bleak and shabby as its surroundings. NB pugs leaving with their branch trains were obliged to pick their way past the coal-strewn clutter of Kinneil Colliery sidings before tackling the stiff gradient which led up past Manuel and on to Polmont. Branch trains climbed unassisted, but freight trains were banked from the rear, with usually a J36 fore and aft.

Back on the main line Linlithgow came next. The viaduct here required gentle negotiation, for after nearly a century's use the fabric was causing concern. Further along, at Philpstoun, a second viaduct warranted equal caution. My father used always to point out the source of the ground subsidence, far below. 'See the old shale working?' he would inquire. I always nodded understandingly, and hoped no one would be so tactless as to ask me what 'shale' was.

Winchburgh, Gogar and Ratho, next three stations, all tucked in rocky gorges, were so undistinguished that bus competition in later years easily foresaw their closure. It was about here we used to catch our first sight of the Forth bridge, when the top halves of two southernmost spans reared quite suddenly above the flat countryside. Even at a distance one was left in no doubt as to the immense size of the structure. The spans were sometimes grey in colour, sometimes red, depending on their state of re-painting. In Scotland the phrase 'like painting the Forth bridge' well described any task we found unending.

APPROACH TO EDINBURGH

A second, and final, glimpse of the mighty bridge was obtained when, between Ratho and Haymarket, the NB's Aberdeen line swept in to accompany us into Edinburgh. One looked sharply up the Aberdeen line with two motives: to spot the bridge, and watch for signs of life at the RAF's Turnhouse aerodrome—for even in the late 1920s an aircraft in flight drew wondering eyes.

After this things began to happen with increasing rapidity. The NB branch line to Corstorphine looped away left, then the spot was reached where Caley trains forsook NB running powers and moved away towards Princes Street. Now Murrayfield's rugby stadium loomed left. The excitement its appearance caused me emanated from no love of rugby, but from the knowledge that Haymarket shed lay immediately beyond. It was a wonderful shed, for, apart from a few wagons which straggled in front, one's view was quite unimpaired. Gresley Pacifics monopolised the eastern end of the shed, while lesser fry, if such a phrase might be employed to embrace a locomotive collection which included a pair of Reid's proud Atlantics, congregated at the other.

Haymarket's platforms had a subterranean gloom about them which made the tunnel ahead almost welcome: then once clear one emerged into a brilliant and sharply contrasted world, and Edinburgh's charm was revealed. Solid rock piled high on the right, while on the left there flourished the fresh beauty of Princes Street gardens, complimented by a backcloth of gaily coloured tramcars as they sailed sedately in shoals along Princes Street itself. One final sortie through Mound tunnel and we were running into Waverley, aiming either for the Up Main, or one of the terminal platforms.

8

Edinburgh Waverley

WAVERLEY! What can one say that might convey its true magic! To record, for instance, that its glass-roofed area occupied 11½ acres does so little to conjure the vast intimacy of the place; for it was a fact that once inside that great glasshouse one was rendered completely immune to the outside world. Nothing could be seen, on one side, of Edinburgh Old Town, with its alleys and piled houses reeking of John Knox and Scottish history, or of the more sedate and spacious New Town on the other. Even the major road link which joined them, the graceful sloping North bridge, sailed over Waverley, much too high above the ravine to establish contact at railway level.

The North British Railway Co, partly inspired by the beauty of Princes Street, partly frustrated by the figure of 42ft which had been imposed by authority as a maximum permissible height for Waverley's glass roofs, had asserted its pride by building Waverley hotel on a grand scale, complete with Gothic clock tower which soared nearly 200ft above ground level. At the west end of the station Waverley bridge connected Old and New towns at more conventional level, and twin carriage ramps running therefrom into Waverley station had the effect of truncating one or two of the terminal platforms.

Yet for such an ambitious station—it was the largest in the country in its day—Waverley was oddly reticent in its provision of passenger exits. Apart from the modest pedestrian facilities which accompanied the carriage ramps leading to and from Waverley bridge, the sole alternative left to passengers wishing

95

to venture from the main central island upon which they invariably found themselves deposited was to take to the spidery footbridge which rambled across the width of the station. On the south side stairs led without ceremony straight into Old Town. Similar stairs existed on the north side of the station, but here, very often, raged the fiercest and coldest wind in Christendom. Ropes, thoughtfully provided by the railway company, did something to alleviate the poor traveller's distress as he levered himself up to the level of Princes Street, but flying umbrellas and hats were a regular, and uproarious, feature of life at Waverley Steps.

Waverley station was really a massive island, at the heart of which were sited offices, booking hall, even signal boxes. Fifteen terminal platforms sprang from this central core, but more imposing were the two through platforms which flanked either side of the main installation. The Down Main impressed by aspiring in length to 1,567ft, but the Up Main exceeded even this by 40ft; 1,607ft—five times the length of a football pitch! So enormous was the latter that even when the *Flying Scotsman* already occupied sixteen or seventeen coach lengths it was common practice for an Aberdeen or Glasgow connection to pull in behind and deposit its London-bound passengers. For them, changing trains merely meant walking further down the platform.

Although the two ends of Waverley were set in equally dramatic surroundings each, nevertheless, had its own distinctive railway character. I have only to think of Waverley's west end to recall the high ornamental balustrades which still flank Waverley bridge, and how as a very small boy I loved to peer through them at traffic below.

Waverley's west end could be surprisingly quiet at times, but if I were in luck, and arrival of a train from the south was imminent, three or four connecting trains, each with a locomotive alert and simmering at its head, would be in position at the various platforms. And here was a sight, for in those days all NB passenger engines wore green. The connection for Aberdeen took prime importance and, lord of all it surveyed, a Reid Atlantic sat with immense panache at its head. Occasionally, if the load were extra heavy, a small NB 4-4-0 would swank additionally in front, next to the coaches, where the NB believed pilot engines properly belonged. Fife and Glasgow connections, not to be outdone, contrived to cut a dash of their own—for the Scotts which headed them were incapable of suppressing their built-in look of whippets anxious to slip the lead and be off. Once the East Coast train arrived and the connections filled up, and much frenzied guard whistling saw them on their various ways, the west end of Waverley subsided gently into quieter habits. Thoroughly refreshed by the wonder of it all I went on my way rejoicing.

The massive turreted edifice which, bedrocked on a lower echelon of Calton Hill, glowered over Waverley's east end must have been mistaken so often for Edinburgh Castle by innocent visitors. The site, happily enough, is now occupied by Scottish government offices, but in the days I speak of Calton gaol it was which squatted there so grimly. As a boy I confess it completely escaped my understanding how punishment could enter into the scheme of things if a man occupied a cell whose window overlooked the east end of Waverley station!

There was, though, *nearly* a grain of truth in this romantic conception, for Waverley's east end was so hemmed in by barriers, natural and otherwise, that normal railway observation was none too easily accomplished, unless one was already on a platform awaiting departure. Trouble was, on the south side a large goods depot thrust itself between public and railway, tracks heading east from Waverley's many platforms funnelled promptly towards Calton tunnel, while on the remaining, north, side the formidable outcrop of rock which supported Calton gaol hardly encouraged picnic parties. All very daunting, until the midsummer of 1930 when Adam's father, determined to record the *Flying Scotsman*'s departure, found his own photographic solution, a steep narrow staircase called Jacob's Ladder which wound its way down to street level from the heights above Calton tunnel.

There was always something happening at Waverley's east end. Routine arrivals and departures apart, a handful of station pilots, ex-NB J class tanks, spent their days fussing about with empty stock, sometimes scuttling, light, clean through the great station as if life itself depended on their fleetness of foot. Other times they snoozed unashamedly at the foot of Calton gaol. But the really soul-stirring feature of life at the east end of Waverley was the morning exodus of southbound expresses I have already described: for here was part of Edinburgh city's daily ritual. So skilfully, in fact, was the affair directed that one did not even require to attend Waverley to savour the drama—for long before the magic hour of ten, and further west at Haymarket, a prologue began to unwind itself almost at break of day.

I can just recall the era when a brace of NE Atlantics handled the *Flying Scotsman,* but memories warm as I focus my mind further on to that wonderful summer of 1933 when the 'Flyer's' non-stop activities between Edinburgh and King's Cross were entrusted exclusively to two Gresley Pacifics, Nos 2795 *Call Boy* and 2796 *Spearmint.* Visit Haymarket shed as early as you cared and one of these two supremely beautiful machines would be poised outside, already immaculate but still being polished and cosseted by a small army of cleaners. The atmosphere at Haymarket was stiff with pride—and in my experience only Grantham depot ever matched their famous stud of green Pacifics.

Eventually, and almost grudgingly, *Spearmint,* if she it was, had to be released for the road. With a certain amount of studied fuss she would be eased out on to the main line, whence she set off, running light, for Waverley. Once through Haymarket tunnel she was well in the public eye and I imagine precious few citizens perambulating in Princes Street gardens at that time of the morning required the evidence of her headboard to convince them that this graceful green apparition, full of steam and swishing lazy clouds of it at rail level ahead of her, was bound on no common errand.

On towards Waverley she would swagger. At the west end of the station crowds would flock to the railings to witness her entry, and her driver and fireman must have been proud men as she steamed across that great arena, to slip quietly in behind cover of her own train and await further orders. Meanwhile, on

Waverley's Up Main platform a considerable audience accumulated about the front end of the train, waiting impatiently for 'the engine to arrive'. Having already identified the Pacific which lay quietly behind I used to chuckle at the speculation which went on around me. Came 9.40, and all were admitted to the secret; for in an atmosphere vibrant with excitement the lovely green locomotive would emerge slowly out into the sunshine, pause, and back gently on to her train. Admirers descended upon her, and the great daily drama one never tired of was well under way.

ST MARGARETS SHED

Locomotives working west of Edinburgh were charged to Haymarket shed, as were those which handled *main line* passenger traffic on the East Coast route. All other engines, goods and passenger, working east were stationed at the NB's secondary depot, St Margarets, a mile or so east of Waverley.

St Margarets seemed to me to achieve miracles in atrociously cramped conditions. It, too, was hemmed in from all sides, and as well as being terminal it suffered acutely from the sooty kind of claustrophobia which, I was to discover later, plagued Camden. Yet despite the murk and gloom one could always observe an immaculately groomed Reid Atlantic lording it amongst other less eye-catching companions. Here, of course, resided all locomotives operating the Waverley route to Carlisle. Despite the congestion there was invariably a line of locomotives to be seen from a passing train, strung along in front of the shed in various states of disrepair. It was, into the bargain, the only *split* shed I ever encountered in Scotland, for on the other side of the main line stood a small roundhouse. Obviously of greater vintage than the main establishment, only vestiges of a roof remained above narrow stone archways, and here were stabled up to a dozen NB 0-4-0 saddle tanks, engines which spent their entire energies working around Leith docks.

THE CALEDONIAN IN EDINBURGH

Edinburgh's third major shed, that at Dalry Road, was the Caley's stronghold; though the dominance the Caley enjoyed over the NB in Glasgow was completely reversed where Edinburgh was concerned. Waverley *was* Edinburgh, and apart from some brisk suburban activity the Caley slipped pretty quietly in and out of the city. With no direct route to London available there was little else they could do. Dock work at Leith and Granton was shared equitably with the NB, but when it came to passenger traffic the Caledonian had never a hope of matching the NB's powerful network.

Not surprisingly Dalry Road shed reflected this inferiority. Fair sized, but rather nondescript, it lacked the glamour of Haymarket and could not approach St Margarets in variety. Essentially Caledonian in character its range of occupants ran little beyond Caley 4-4-0s, 0-6-0s and a Compound or two. Its quota of tank engines bore scrutiny, though, for, apart from a nucleus of McIntosh class 1P 0-4-4 tanks designed specially for suburban work and known as the Cathcart, or Balerno, class, it embraced two of Fowler's post-grouping 0-6-0 Dock tanks. These were delightful little objects. Short wheel based and deeply outside-cylindered they bore five-digit numbers from the Lancashire & Yorkshire range in their early days. I admired them greatly and was anxious to photograph one, but fate ordained this should never happen. Any time I passed the shed and one was standing outside, I was sans camera; while any time I visited the shed, armed with camera, one was either buried inside, or both were out working in the docks. Decades have passed, and the deficiency still rankles.

The Caley's Edinburgh terminus, Princes Street, though grossly overshadowed by Waverley contrived bravely to present a bold public front. It incorporated very handsomely its own hotel, and once inside one could not but be impressed by the spaciousness of the station. Yet somehow the terminus lacked vitality, and there was ever present that air of quiet melancholy which pervaded Marylebone and St Pancras.

Still, it had its moments of glory: witness the summer of 1928 when on 28 April, four days before the *Flying Scotsman* was due to introduce its devastating non-stop schedule between King's Cross and Edinburgh, the LMS pulled off a tactical masterstroke by quietly running the *Royal Scot* in two portions, *both* non-stop, to Glasgow and Edinburgh respectively. A Royal Scot *Cameronian*, handled the eight coaches destined for Glasgow, while, of all things, a *Compound* took six coaches to Edinburgh.

That must have been quite a day for LMS staff when No 1054 rolled into Princes Street, travel stained, her tender empty, her footplate crammed to suffocation with train crew and observers. Unsung, but completely victorious! Her achievement was a vainglorious one, I suppose, in that it could not possibly have been perpetuated in public service. But surely a feat of this calibre by a 4-4-0 must rank as one of the most gallant, and gruelling, efforts in British railway history.

Certainly rumour hath it that 'e'en the ranks of Tuscany could scarce forbear to cheer . . . '.

9
Visits to Perth

IN the early days it hardly mattered to Adam and myself that, because of our Falkirk domicile, locomotives of the one time Highland railway escaped our attentions. The central Scottish activities of the NB and Caledonian employed hundreds of locomotives, and yielded interest and excitement enough to satisfy the appetite of any two railway-loving youngsters. Then, inevitably, curiosity overcame us, and by August 1934 we had resolved it was high time we made physical acquaintance with the Highland. Accordingly, an expedition to Perth, the nearest point of contact, was planned.

Off we set from Grahamston early one Saturday morning. At Larbert we bundled out of the branch train in high spirits, for the morning sun held promise, and soon our Perth train rolled in. Much to our delight it had two Caley 4-4-0s at its head. A careful choice of seat as near the engines as possible and we were on our way.

Stirling shed was only 8 miles distant. The Royal blue which once fired my imagination no longer graced the scene, but there remained little doubt as to who ruled the roost, for each of the dozen locos in sight was Caledonian. North of the station a reciprocal state of independence existed at the LNER shed, and the smaller coterie of engines which quietly minded their business there was NB to a man. These we found a particularly rewarding proposition, for their normal daily activities took them into Clackmannanshire and deep into Fife, well tucked away from number-seeking enthusiasts based on Falkirk.

APPROACH TO PERTH

I imagine the first sight of a new large shed has much the same effect on railway enthusiasts the world over. We had hardly emerged from Moncrief tunnel, a mile or so south of Perth, when the Caledonian shed put in an appearance on our left. We were passing briskly and the mass of engines on shed was none too easy to segregate, thus my resultant gyrations may well have given my companion cause to fear I might somersault clean through the carriage window in my excitement. Anticipating no doubt I might follow up with a request that my feet be held while I ventured farther from the compartment Adam focused his usual calm on the proceedings by reminding me, a shade tartly, that Perth South shed was unlikely to be dismantled within the next hour or so. I was still considering the logic of his observation when the LNER shed swam into view, and could not help noting a little gleefully that Adam moved quickly enough to join me in admiring the scenery.

Our main concern once a lightning reconnaissance of Perth General station had been accomplished was to pinpoint the Highland shed. We tackled an elderly porter on the subject, but as luck would have it he himself was Highland, and his advice, though well meant, was so larded with 'ochs' and 'tur-rns' we were little the wiser by the end of it. Falling back on instinct we steered a course over the main railway bridge. There, facing a long wooden platform used for Perth Hunt traffic, stood Perth North shed. A certain amount of smoke hung about, vouching that life existed, and we quickly descended to the wooden platform— only to find that a line of stationary vans and wagons strung across in front of the shed denied us a preview. As if to tax our patience further, a main line signal dropped.

I think had not Adam counselled more wisely I should have opted for a smart dash across the quadruple-tracked main line, for the invisible contents of the shed were vexing me sorely. After all, as I pointed out severely to my friend, somewhere behind these wretched wagons lay our first Highland engines. Adam had the perfect answer. He nudged me in mid-protest and nodded mutely in the direction of Perth General station. There, coasting at the head of a goods train as if she had all day, a Jones Goods slowly approached. Not only our first Highland engine—but Britain's pioneer 4-6-0 class into the bargain!

Frantically I fumbled for my camera. No 17929 had not really altered much in forty years. Her originally louvred chimney had given way to one of Drummond character, and conventional Ross pop safety valves had supplanted the tall twin columns favoured by David Jones; but all else, the Stroudleyesque cab, tender, sandboxed leading splasher, the handrail looping oddly over the smokebox, remained. Having broken Highland ice with such devastating effect we wasted little time in scuttling across the tracks.

PERTH NORTH SHED

First glimpse behind the barricades maintained excitement at high level. Two locomotives were readily apparent. A Horwich 2-6-0 stood nose out on one road, while next to her a great River 4-6-0, fully emerged, was being groomed for active service. It was 14757; an even more distinguished find than we realised at the time, for later research revealed her to be *River Spey* (though, of course, she never bore the name), one of the ill-starred pair delivered at F. G. Smith's behest to the Highland railway back in 1916.

Even by Caledonian standards she was big. On top of a broad Belpaire firebox and massively smokeboxed boiler squatted a dome of commensurate proportions, and certainly the most generously flared chimney Adam and I had ever seen. At the cab end the River's high main frame, with its distinctive twin splasher, dropped to meet an eight-wheeled tender, sheer sided as a coach and demonstrably the largest and heaviest in the country in its day. As an NB man, my heart could not but go out to the Highland. What a blow to lose an engine like this—and to the Caley of all people!

Thrilled at having captured two new Highland types within a space of five minutes we addressed ourselves with relish to a third, for right alongside lurked further treasure—14768 *Clan Mackenzie*. More modestly proportioned than her immediate

104

stable companion, and black now as opposed to the dark green livery of Highland days, the Cumming engine still looked handsome, and immediate impressions deemed her a really sophisticated design; though, of course, Adam and I had no illusions as to the power and tenacity which lay beneath that bland exterior. Her substantial outside cylinders and delicate valve gear were rendered unobtrusive and part of a flowing design by the employment of valence and splashers, a practice we had already encountered on locomotives of the NE and LNW. Her square-topped firebox merged into a fine broad cab whose deep protective roof swept back right to the tender.

Full marks to Cumming. She was a lovely engine. Only one snag presented itself. We could not get at her with our cameras, for she was completely screened by the River's great bulk. This annoying state defied every contortion we could think of, and stalemate seemed certain, when fate intervened in the shape of the River's driver.

I doubt if the poor chap ever had a pair of friendly vultures descend on him before, but so cordial was our greeting, and so cunning our conversation, he probably never realised the critical import of his remark that while he and the River were about to quit the shed, the *Clan* was not due out for another hour or so. Restored of heart we bade farewell and strolled off to have a closer look at that Horwich 2-6-0; for the number she bore accorded oddly with the five-digit numbers we already knew. No mistake, though. Her number really was 2913. The LMS, we suspected, were almost as capable as the LNER of getting up to tricks in their numbering, but in the absence of specific knowledge there was little we could do but shrug our shoulders. Later that morning No 13206 rolled into the yard and succeeded in thoroughly reconfusing the whole issue.

Presently the River kept faith, left the shed, and disappeared in the direction of Perth General. Our vigil at an end, we closed in on *Clan Mackenzie*. This appeared to exhaust shed prospects for the time being. Adam's encyclopaedic instincts with timetables warned of impending departures, so our next move lay in getting back across the lines to the wooden platform. Over on the platform we settled down patiently and waited. For a while nothing happened. Then followed the kind of activity which made railway observation in the 1930s such a delight.

MORNING RUSH HOUR

The first departure ran true to form. It was our old friend the River, looking positively out of character with stopping passenger headlamp, taking out the 9.30 to Inverness. The driver, recognising his former inquisitors, saluted. Without giving offence, we hoped, we carefully completed our photographs before responding. Poor *Spey*, we had no way of knowing, but she was to be the first River to go. In fact both she and the Jones Goods we had seen earlier went to the scrapyard in 1936. Within minutes of the River's passing the same signal dropped again. What now? we wondered.

Very shortly, chuffing gently towards us at the head of a two-coach 9.40 to Blair Atholl, came a remarkable answer—our first Highland 4-4-0, No 14382 *Loch Moy*. I am sure I stood there open mouthed as she approached, for she was an odd sight. While (as with the Jones Goods) the hand of David Jones could not be concealed, her general appearance nevertheless had undergone radical transformation at one time or another. Despite a certain dumpiness in her deportment the trick was highly effective, for the vision of outside cylinders on what, from a distance, seemed certain to be a Caledonian 4-4-0 so bemused my faculties that I was much too late in raising my camera.

Fortunately Adam kept his wits about him, and *Loch Moy* was safely recorded. Of interest in his picture are two typically Jones touches, the unusual pear-shaped glasses in front of her cab and the hinged vacuum pillar whereby the vacuum pipe was folded back flat on the front buffer beam when not in use. She carried, too, a number plate on her smokebox, and in accordance with general Scottish practice her name was painted on the leading splasher. One of Jones's original fifteen Lochs she looked, I must say, remarkably trim for a locomotive dating back to 1896.

Certainly she presented a more modern appearance than the younger engine which followed her on stage; appropriately

(*above*) LNER No 2910 and LMS No 14625 (ex-CR Pickersgill Oban bogie No 197) meet at Larbert in July 1935; (*below*) a family of McIntosh tanks at Fouldubs shed, Grangemouth, in June 1935. Left to right they are LMS Nos 16375, 15142 and 16164—CR Nos 395, 884 and 538

page 108
LMS No 17908 (ex-CR McIntosh superheated goods 4-6-0 No 182 built in 1913) heads a Glasgow–Crieff holiday express of very assorted stock through Larbert in August 1934

enough, Peter Drummond's variation on a four-coupled theme, his Small Ben. Long before we could identify the actual locomotive we recognised the family hallmarks on the 4-4-0 which now approached us at the head of a short goods train. Here we stood on familiar ground, for, viewed externally, only her rather more stylish chimney and strange eight-wheeled tender (of which more presently) precluded the stranger from being vintage Caledonian. No Stroudley echoes either about the cab. It, too, was pure Drummond. It turned out to be 14410 *Ben Dearg*.

Despite Highland blandishments the greatest surprise that morning was yet to come. It arrived in the form of a goods train which passed soon after. Adam and I knew a Great Central ex-ROD 2-8-0 well enough when we saw one, but the thought had not entered our heads that the Highland main line might test our powers of observation in that direction. Yet there, quite undeniably, she was: No 6544 of the breed, still flaunting her shapely Robinson chimney, her small driving wheels gripping hard as she urged her train northwards. So intrigued were we by the unlikely event it did not even occur to us to wonder where on earth she was going. As it happened she must have been delivering to some nearby yard, for not long after she reappeared, as did the Jones Goods, running back south with a few wagons and a van; and with this final flourish the morning 'rush' from Perth ended.

SECOND HIGHLAND THOUGHTS

The Caley shed at Perth South now beckoned powerfully. We were free to wander as we wished, yet Adam and I detected in each other a marked reluctance to leave the Highland scene. Compromise was selected. One more look behind the barricades, then off we must go. Back across the lines we trudged.

Out instincts proved sound. Unbeknown to us *Beaufort Castle* had emerged, and now stood unattended outside the shed. Almost forty years have passed, and I still cannot make up my mind about that engine. Seeing one's first Castle was no mean event, but from the outset I found these 4-6-0s the most difficult of all Highland classes to assess. I mean aesthetically, of course. There never was any doubt as to their capabilities.

The trouble was, for a legendary locomotive the Castle looked so *rugged*. A tall Drummond chimney and gaunt squarish dome endowed her with a distinctly elderly, and rather melancholy, Caledonian air. As with the Loch here, too, was something of a confidence trick, for despite the provision of a Drummond cab and double splasher a strong family resemblance to the Jones Goods betrayed itself at footplate level and above.

Perhaps it was a pity I had to view my first Castle with a Clan lounging elegantly alongside. Perhaps, too, my initial disappointment caused me to react a little unchivalrously, but neither did I find myself attracted to her eight-wheeled tender. Anticipating later (Dugald) Drummond practice on the LSW it had been designed with inside wheel bearings. The theory was, I understand, that this facilitated re-use of spare bogie wheels. A fair Scottish argument, I dare say; but one which on this occasion failed to commend itself. To *my* Scottish soul the sight of four naked wheels ranged side by side beneath a tender seemed almost indecent; rather like a row of human teeth overgenerously exposed. In any case, inside bearings must have been the very devil to tolerate when repairs or maintenance were called for.

Adam and I were still brooding on the subject when *Clan Mackenzie* and the Horwich 2-6-0 quit the shed together and disappeared stationwards. Our stubbornness in trekking once more back to the wooden platform was amply rewarded when the two engines charged jointly out of Perth General, heading the 11.55 express to Inverness. No 2913 led in front as if she had worked the Highland line all her life.

Back at Perth General station calm had descended now that main-line activity had waned. A McIntosh 4-4-0 mooned around, trailing a van as if looking for a suitable place to jettison it. At the southern end the only other object in sight, the station pilot, a Caledonian 4-4-0 Lambie tank, openly rested. She could not rise to the sheer pertness of her NB Edinburgh equivalent, but she was a tidy object just the same. Eleven years after grouping, her faded maroon livery made a brave show and it was refreshing to see again the once-familiar LMS crest.

Further south the Reid Atlantic, which earlier that morning had basked in sunshine outside the NB shed, had vanished. One could assume she was by now well on her way to Edinburgh. Sole survivors, an NB class M 4-4-0 poking tender first from the small shed, and one superheated 0-6-0 lifeless inside, placed no obstacle in our way, and we moved on towards the Caley shed.

PERTH SOUTH SHED

Life here was largely as might have been expected. We were aware that down south a gentleman called Stanier was making his presence felt in LMS circles, but so far Scotland had not felt the impact of his personality, and native locomotives grappling with increasingly heavy traffic drew what assistance was necessary from Fowler LMS types: Compounds, 2-6-0s and 2Ps in the main. Perth South was no exception. Apart from a sprinkling of Compounds and 2-6-0s everything in the shed was Caledonian. There were dozens of them: 0-6-0 tanks, 0-4-4 tanks, all three types of 0-6-0 tender engine, and, to handle the cream of passenger traffic, a representative range of McIntosh and Pickersgill 4-4-0s. The absence of Caley 4-6-0s did not escape us and had, we feared, an ominous ring about it. The very profuseness of the scene was tempting, but practical considerations in the form of absence of sun intervened. After considerable heart searching we put our cameras away, having decided the sky had clouded over too permanently to warrant the expenditure of valuable film on subjects we might as easily obtain at Larbert.

Sun or no sun, commonsense was to triumph over economic instinct when two outstanding exceptions came our way. Both locos were so rare I am sure we should have 'shot' them in semi-darkness if need be. First to appear was 14618, ex-Caledonian 908 class, a 5ft 9in mixed traffic 4-6-0 introduced by McIntosh in 1906; a big handsome engine whose roomy double-windowed cab bore large serriffed numerals of a type I do not remember seeing on any other Scottish engine. Ten of the class had passed into LMS hands in 1923. Two even bore famous names—*Sir James King* and *Barochan*—but the names soon disappeared and the pair perished anonymously with others in the early 1930s. No 14618 that day at Perth was the first and last of the type I saw. By 1936 all had gone.

Memories of the second odd man out make happier reading. They are of 14010, the last single wheeler to run in the country. We hardly noticed the Caley 4-2-2 at first, for she had quietly assumed a place amongst a line of working locomotives. This she was perfectly entitled to do, for she was still performing daily between Perth and Dundee. Poor old lady, she looked rather grimy. She had not yet become a *cause célèbre*, and certainly we had no inkling of the glamorous future which lay before her. Nor, I imagine, did many other folk. Doggedly, despite the murky sky overhead, we photographed her.

So it was in Perth in 1934. So intrigued were Adam and I by the new railway world revealed, we vowed to return. We kept that vow, in successive years. But things were never quite the same.

PERTH REVISITED

By May 1935 the Lambie station pilot had gone, and in her place dallied a Caley 0-4-4 tank, neither maroon nor half so dainty. The NB shed had perked up, though, and made amends for its poor showing the year before. Outside in the sun Reid Atlantic No 9904, newly arrived from Edinburgh, displayed her green livery to maximum advantage. Company habits were dying hard at Perth, for like *Glen Lyon*, who brought the next NB train in, *Holyrood* still bore on top of her smokebox a familiar curved red and white indicator board, inscribed 'Perth'. Representative of the new school, 246 *Morayshire* emerged gracefully from the small shed to work a train back the other way.

Where LMS sheds were concerned each had its own tale to tell. That of Perth North was a sorry one. But for one Castle tucked disconsolately inside, the shed was empty. Outside in the yard 13107, still stolidly perpetuating the Crab numbering mystery, prepared for duty.

Perth South, too, seemed less congested than before; but here, at least, were compensations. The first loco in sight, 14628, one of the Caley class 60 4-6-0s I admired so much, posed leisurely before moving off to admit in her place, No 5013. A new Stanier

Mixed Traffic 4-6-0! Heavens, what a day! Some of the first batch of Staniers had been sent north to relieve chronic Scottish traffic pressures, and only a week or two previously their initial appearance at Larbert had caused quite a commotion. Here was a chance to examine one at close range. So commonplace has the class become since, it is well nigh impossible to resummon the awe with which, forty years ago, we approached the 'original article'. I took to the engine and was greatly impressed by her appearance. Oddly enough, though I have photographed countless Staniers since I have never succeeded in capturing the powerful lines of Stanier's design more eloquently than I did that afternoon in May 1935.

DISTINGUISHED VISITOR

Even with that scalp on our belts the day was to finish on a higher note. As we trudged back to Perth General we observed a train was signalled on the platform which swoops in so grandly from the east. Expecting nothing more than a Caledonian 4-4-0 we lingered, as always, on principle—and were dumbfounded when a mighty vision in crimson rolled in at the head of a train from Dundee—6156 *The South Wales Borderer*! Adam and I looked blankly at each other—a Royal Scot *north* of *Glasgow*!—then out came our cameras to record the historic event. In our minds swam the parallel of *William Whitelaw*'s classic debut at Falkirk High years before. As in the case of the LNER Pacific a few more months was to see the extraordinary accepted as routine practice; but no passage of time, I am glad to say, can erode in my memory the wonder and poignancy of two great occasions.

FINAL VISIT TO PERTH

Our last reconnaissance was made in August 1936. By now the situation on the Highland was more obscure than ever. Clans, we were happily aware, had been transferred to the Oban line, but the fate which had befallen Castles, Lochs and Bens was anyone's guess.

Even then Perth South shed tried hard to please. Sandwiched in line between a Drummond 0-6-0 and a Royal Scot, a large inside-cylindered Caley 4-6-0 offered every likelihood of being another *Sir James King*, but turned out instead to be 17910, one of eleven 179 class freight locomotives built by McIntosh just before the eruption of World War I. Although some time before I had bagged a picture of 17908 heading a Crieff train through Larbert, a second bite at the same cherry was not to be despised.

Also flanked by a Royal Scot—changed times, indeed, at Perth—a second Caley surprise awaited us: 2-6-0 No 17804. This would have been a great capture, had we not stumbled across our first of the class earlier that month at Motherwell. The total class, built in 1912, consisted of five engines only. The Perth engine, 17804, only just outlived the others and was herself withdrawn in 1937. Further indicative of changed times one solitary Jubilee presented itself: 5584, unnamed as yet, maroon, neat— yet not, to my eyes, as impressive as Stanier's MT locomotive. Provision of splashers over the driving wheels heightened an already marked affinity to Great Western design, and certainly made for a tidy sophisticated appearance. But the unabashedly powerful look of her black sisters made the greater impact on me.

Sadly, I can find no record of having seen a Highland loco-motive at Perth that autumn day in 1936. They were, as I shall presently relate, by no means finished as far as I was concerned; but each time I probe mentally for my last recollection of a Highland engine on its native soil I find myself redirected to that wan memory of a Castle slumbering inside Perth North shed. Yet only twelve months earlier the same shed had yielded acute pleasure.

The moral which commends itself is one of thankfulness that I was privileged to visit Perth before the last of the great days were over.

10

The Glasgow & Sou' West

AFTER grouping in 1923 it rapidly became apparent that locomotive classes small in number were unloved by authority. Understandably they were much less economic to maintain than the large
classes of standard types which were being introduced, and
enthusiasts grieved as well-loved solitary types began to disappear.
If only because of the chaotic state of that system's motive
power, LMS engines were particularly vulnerable. Glasgow &
South Western locomotives in particular, 528 strong when the
LMS took over but hopelessly diffuse in character, paid the small-
class penalty with a vengeance. Class after class began to vanish,
as the Scots might put it, like 'snaw aff a dyke'. The process
gained momentum into the 1930s, and Midland influence, now
expressed as official LMS policy in the shape of Compounds and
standard class 2P 4-4-0s, penetrated so deeply all over the SW
system that soon the two types had gained a near monopoly on all
passenger traffic.

ST ENOCH STATION

My first real contact with the G & SW was not made until May
1935, when on an impulse I spent a Saturday afternoon at St
Enoch station. By evening I was wishing I had gone there before,
for from a photographic and aesthetic point of view it proved
easily the best of the Glasgow termini.

St Enoch contrived somehow to escape the claustrophobic
atmosphere of the other three and offered that railway phenomenon, rare in Glasgow: a pleasing spacious vista. Its domed

glass-roofed area was neat in appearance and moderate enough in size to permit long platforms to curve out gracefully into open space, whence the southbound lines gathered themselves majestically for a wide rightward sweep towards the River Clyde. St Enoch's platforms lay at an angle of 90° to those of its near neighbour and rival, Glasgow Central, but the two stations' exits by bridge over the Clyde contrived to be parallel, and quite close.

Even when in 1934 Stanier began to pour out his new 4-6-0s only a few Jubilees gravitated at first towards the west. That day, for instance, I walked into St Enoch in 1935 I counted six class 2Ps and three Compounds at work before a Jubilee finally showed up, and No 5621 backed in to take charge of a St Pancras express. Nameless as yet, but later to become *Northern Rhodesia*, she looked a pretty picture as she steamed out, maroon and highly polished, at the head of her train. More 2Ps arrived and left, and as a delightful afternoon slipped past the only disturbing factor was the continued absence of G & SW locomotives. I knew they were becoming scarce, but this was hair raising.

Presently even the sight of a familiar looking 0-6-0 running in tender first raised hopes, but the straw proved hardly worth clutching. It was only 17421, one of the legions of Caley Drummonds. She pottered about for a while, then drifted over to the one-time St Enoch locomotive shed which lay opposite, bounded by a triangle of main lines. Soon she had company. Compound No 1132, red and gleaming, joined her in the sun.

For a while I studied the two engines, and found myself thinking what superb machines the Compounds were, just to look at. I had by now seen many pre-grouping locomotives but nothing in my experience had weakened an early-formed conviction that engines of the Great Northern and Midland Railways were the noblest of them all. Both railways' locomotives may have been modest in character (Gresley's later contributions excepted) but to me they never failed to exude an air of charm and efficiency. The front ends in particular were immaculately conceived. A Midland or GN smokebox always *looked* right. No 1132, undisputedly Midland in character despite her LMS parentage, certainly looked a lady of quality that afternoon; so much so that for the first time I found myself responding with sympathy to her English nickname, 'Crimson Rambler'.

Now this was interesting, for in Scotland we had never developed the use of nicknames to any extent. Do not misunderstand me; soubriquets of great variety were employed by Scottish enginemen towards all sorts of locomotive—and these covered, I may say, the expected range of emotions—but most Scotsmen shrank by nature from use of the affectionate or diminutive. Thus, when my visit to London in 1934 unearthed such specimens of the genre as 'Crimson Rambler', 'Jinty' and 'Crab', I found myself shying a little self-consciously from their use. 1132 performed a service that day by curing me of my diffidence. It was not long before I and my friend Adam had cheerfully incorporated other English names into our routine railway conversation.

Still absorbed in admiring the Compounds I nearly missed the first great event of the day. There were sounds of an approaching train. I looked round casually, rather expecting another class 2P, and nearly dropped my camera as a large ungainly engine rounded the bend smartly with a train from Paisley. Merciful heavens, a Glasgow & Sou' West engine! Just in time I snapped her as she sailed in, and got her number—17821. She turned out to be one of eleven 2-6-0s built to Drummond's design by the NB Locomotive Co in 1915. My initial, though hasty, assessment of her as 'strange' was, alas, substantiated when her coaches were removed and she followed out slowly into the open. Massively built, for she was scaled in the true Peter Drummond tradition, she still could not conceal the uncommonly awkward look of an ordinary 0-6-0 which had had its footplate extended to take a pony truck. With the best will in the world I could not bring myself to dub her a handsome locomotive.

Had I but known, Peter Drummond was not to be the only purveyor of shocks that afternoon. His successor, R. H. Whitelegg, too, had something pretty potent up his sleeve. Evidence was forthcoming not much later when, lurching round the bend on an incoming Kilmarnock train, there appeared the most remarkable locomotive I had yet clapped eyes on. A Midland-style number plate mounted in front of her strangely fashioned smokebox soon resolved the matter of identity. It was No 15403, a G & SW Baltic tank. I think 'tank' was perhaps the operative word, for as she bore down in my direction her great maroon bulk conveyed every likelihood of being some sort of armoured war machine. 99 tons of solid metal—what a scale on which to build tank engines! And what an impression she and her five sisters must have created when they first appeared, garbed in gleaming green, in 1922! Luckily the state of near-hypnosis her appearance induced did not preclude me from photographing her triumphal entry into St Enoch. This accomplished, I decided a closer look at this phenomenon was more than usually justified, and hastened back down the platform.

My first impression on reaching her was that her architect must have had a passion for geometry. I cannot recall seeing another locomotive whose design invoked such a medley of lines, straight edges and curves. Her pedigree was distinctly odd. Viewed from the front there was even a certain resemblance to the LNER Directors I knew so well. Her chimney, for instance, was not dissimilar; neither, though squarer and more severe in shape, was her dome. Her main frame was conceived in much the same sturdy fashion; but here the similarity ended, and consideration of the frontal details which remained placed me firmly, I fear, on the side of Robinson. Not only was her smokebox grossly overclad, but her buffers—neither honestly oval like the Directors, nor round like normal Scottish engines—compromised, rather clumsily I felt, by employing horizontal edges and rounded sides. Perhaps, to my eyes, the most disturbing feature of all was the smokebox door which appeared positively bulbous as it peered from its heavy surrounding collar. A *completely circular* handrail mounted plumb centre thereon, no doubt meant to be decorative, tended rather to revive my earlier misgivings by creating a somewhat unconventional torpedo-tube effect.

Below footplate level one could not cavil. The main frame was not stepped in any way, and the external valve gear was unobtrusively tucked away as in the manner of Claughtons and Clans. The splasher which accommodated the leading driving wheel merged into the sidetank, whereon the number was painted in unmistakable terms. The top edge of the tank was oddly fluted and this tended to lead the eye towards the safety valve which, in turn, was so strangely potlike that when it emitted steam one might have wondered if it was a second chimney. The rear end of the engine embodied precisely the capacious cab and bunker one would have expected from a tank of Baltic dimensions. All in all the predominant feeling which grew on me as I studied this remarkable locomotive was one of mass and dead weight. Powerful and welcome additions to SW express stock they must have been in their day, yet they displayed, I believe, a marked penchant for rolling and developing hot bearings. If this were so I imagine the former vice must have made them a formidable ride for even the most case-hardened Sou' West crew.

That evening details of my visit to St Enoch, and the melancholy intelligence it produced regarding the survival rate of Sou' West locomotives, were duly conveyed to Adam. We were very much preoccupied with thoughts of our impending first trip to London, and rather foolishly we decided further investigation into G & SW territory would have to wait. In the event June 1936 arrived before I found myself back at St Enoch. This time I was in Adam's company and we held permits for Corkerhill and Hurlford sheds.

ST ENOCH—JUNE 1936

Half an hour's observation at St Enoch produced little evidence of change. 2Ps and Compounds buzzed about, and Sou' West engines were conspicuous as ever by their absence. Even the sight of a Jubilee at the head of a London express seemed normal; until we moved in to photograph her departure and found that No 5692, in fact, carried a nameplate, inscribed *Cyclops*. Thus we netted our first named Jubilee. This commendable start to the day's proceedings was quickly supplemented. No 17830, another of Drummond's 2-6-0s, drifted in light and obligingly held her pose at the head of an Ayr train while we dashed up and down platforms to get within camera range. Rather a pity, we felt, she was not to haul us to Kilmarnock instead of 650, the almost inevitable 2P which now awaited our pleasure.

We really should have known better than quibble at the prospect of travelling behind a 2P, for we had watched them often enough accelerate smartly away from St Enoch with their five-and six-coach loads. No 650 took pains to rub home the point, for once clear of the Glasgow rail complex she went like the wind. I cannot swear our journey to Kilmarnock was non-stop, but it certainly lived up to the best Sou' West flying traditions. Meanwhile, Adam and I lurched away in a corner seat behind the engine and brazenly enjoyed every moment of the lesson being taught us.

KILMARNOCK AND HURLFORD SHED

Kilmarnock at first sight looked like being a disappointment. Even allowing for the fact it was Saturday afternoon the station seemed quieter than we expected, and what traffic there was seemed to be the exclusive property of class 2Ps. Handsome engines though they were, we were beginning to get just a little tired of the sight of them.

Our next task was to select a route to Hurlford shed which would (accidentally, as it were) cause us to pass Kilmarnock locomotive works on the way. Alas, the works yard that particular afternoon had little to boast of beyond a few Caley 4-4-0s and 0-6-0s. Ironically enough, the sole inhabitant of more than common interest was Highland in origin, 14679 *Blair Castle*; and considering she stood there shorn of pistons, valve gear and coupling rods, it took a considerable act of faith on our parts to persuade ourselves she was in for nothing more lethal than repairs. Increasingly dubious by now as to whether our expedition was really worth while we moved on towards Hurlford shed.

Nothing there looked like relieving our gloom. Compound No 1148 stood nicely enough on the turntable. Adam photographed her, while I confirmed our worst suspicions by establishing that all four locos lined up behind her were 2Ps. The front ends of two more, and a Caledonian 0-6-0, all that could be seen peering from the black depths of the shed, did not augur well for our afternoon's G & SW locomotive hunt. We paused to hold a council of war, unable at heart to blink the fact that if Kilmarnock could not produce a single specimen little hope attached to looking elsewhere. It was then as we stood outside the shed, spirits rapidly sinking, that the miracle occurred, and a *brace* of Sou' West engines quietly emerged!

Adam and I could do little but gawp. We really needed a moment or two to recover from shock, but the dawning fact that the two locomotives were displaying no inclination to loiter lent powerful assistance towards a speedy recovery. Down the yard we raced, cameras in hand, determined to obtain photographs if it meant chasing the pair of them all the way into Kilmarnock. Fortunately our quarry was only teasing, and stopped to pose for us a hundred yards further down. The sun came out to add watery compliments and, breathless but triumphant, we prepared for action.

The leading engine took my mind back a few years. It was my old friend the 0-6-2 tank, whose fleeting appearance at Carlisle in 1929 had me in such sore straits. This time a complete number was visible—16915. One of a class of eighteen built during the years 1915–17, and later augmented in number by Whitelegg, she had what I was beginning to recognise as the Peter Drummond 'four square' look, and appeared substantially enough engineered to have emanated from a marine workshop, much less those of the NB Locomotive Co. Reid's NB 0-6-2 tanks which up to now had formed my (Scottish) criterion suddenly seemed terrier like by comparison.

The 0-6-0 tender engine behind her, 17519, spoke simply of halcyon days on the Sou' West. I had never seen her like before but I knew without prompting she was a creation of James Manson. There was no mistaking that lovely blend of line and curves which had gone into her making. She looked a shade more robust than the GN 4-4-0s I already knew, but the line formed by her shapely chimney, dome, high spring-balanced safety valve and trim cab offered still an object lesson in symmetry. Interestingly, her tender, though much lower than cab roof level as was the fashion of her period, contrived somehow to approach modern LMS practice more closely than that of any other Scottish engine I had seen. The base of her smokebox had once glowed red in front and now bore a coat of fresh black paint. She was, I discovered

121

later, Manson's third class of 0-6-0, and belonged originally to the 361 class, thirty-four of which were constructed during 1900-10. Maryport & Carlisle Railway must have been impressed as well, for they had one locomotive built in 1908 from the same drawings. Meanwhile, in much better form, we pressed on. Who knew what delights Corkerhill might reveal?

CORKERHILL SHED

Poor Corkerhill! Unbeknown to us the running staff there were in no position to entertain guests. An hour later the first sight to greet us as we walked towards the shed was that of 578, a class 2P, heeled over on an approach road at a distinctly unladylike angle, her front end pointing one way, her tender another, as if someone had broken her spine. Her straddled posture across adjoining tracks spoke volumes, and in the process answered a question which had often occupied my youthful curiosity, ie, what happens when a locomotive negotiates points which are wrongly set? A breakdown crane had been brought alongside, and as Adam and I warily circled the scene salvage staff probed and considered remedies. With camera slung at the ready the impulse to record the calamity was strong. The more I prowled round, however, the more I became conscious of embarrassed, rather than hostile, glances from the breakdown staff. I well remember staying my hand in response to twin lines of reasoning which coursed through my head.

The first was positively noble and simply supported the proposition that to perpetuate such an unfortunate moment in LMS affairs would be an act ill becoming a railwayman's son. The second, a mite less altruistic I fear, consisted of a rapid mind's eye view of what might ensue should such a picture somehow reach a newspaper office. No more shed permits—that's what might ensue, I decided grimly—and put my camera away. Meeting Adam as he roamed anticlockwise I acquainted him with my decision and added a brief indication of the solemn elements which had gone into its making. He listened politely, appeared impressed, and moved on.

Two weeks later at his home some freshly processed postcards were passed my way. Most were near duplicates of shots of my own taken at Corkerhill and as such appeared to warrant little comment. Until, that is, I came to the penultimate print, when I found myself looking at a picture of 578, a class 2P, heeled over at a distinctly unladylike angle!

The derailment apart, Corkerhill seemed loath to excite us. We came across a Jubilee, 5637 *Windward Islands,* tucked away in one corner of the yard, but soon the old familiar pattern reasserted itself: 2Ps, 2Ps and more 2Ps. Only in the last line of locomotives we examined did magic break loose; for here, jammed mutely between a 2P and a Sou' West 0-6-2 tank, was hidden a G & SW 4-4-0—14520, a big rangy-looking engine of typically Drummond dimensions. Apart from isolated experiments by Whitelegg six of these locos, class 131, dating from 1913, and a further six, class 137, produced the following two years, represented the G & SW's last word in 4-4-0s. She was not what I would term a handsome locomotive.

We arrived home that evening pleased with our discoveries, but not at all sure the Sou' West had revealed all it should. This uncertainty lingered for the best part of a year, until the arrival of our first *Locomotive Stock Book* shattered the illusion. Truth was, mortality amongst G & SW locomotives since grouping had not been heavy: it had been *cataclysmic!* A 1923 stud of 528 locomotives had been hacked by 31 December 1936 to 36. Of these 21 were 0-6-2 tanks, 7 more were 2-6-0s, and in all only *four* types of locomotive remained. What on earth happened?

Consider for a moment the men who built Scotland's locomotives during the fifty years prior to grouping. To detail the complexities of their relationships within the five companies would require a large volume; but one fact clearly emerges. With the minor exception of the Great North of Scotland, which pursued strangely inbred traditions for its own reasons, the name Drummond features prominently in all their histories. Despite the immense variety of locomotives built, never in the case of the NB and Caley was variety a weakness; for Dugald Drummond laid down a solid foundation of simple locomotive design, and, to a man, his successors pursued their talents within that framework of continuous and traditional development. Holmes, Reid and Chalmers followed the line at Cowlairs; Lambie, McIntosh and Pickersgill added their quota of individualism at St Rollox. Not surprisingly, large classes of 0-6-0 and 4-4-0, built on Drummond bedrock, soldiered on almost until steam itself became redundant.

Six men, all bearing illustrious names, bequeathed the G & SW's complement of locos to 1923 grouping; and what a galaxy of types and rebuilds they left behind! Patrick Stirling, his brother James, Hugh Smellie, James Manson, Peter Drummond, R. H. Whitelegg; it would be difficult to nominate a more widely ranging line of succession where loco-building aesthetics were concerned. Herein, of course, lies the weakness of the SW case, for, Drummond apart and Whitelegg set aside as a late eccentric, none of the others built for *strength* and *durability*. Stirling and Smellie engines, even in 1923 offering a surprising total of 152, were worn out long before amalgamation. Manson's legacy of 293 machines, though it embraced some fine engines, had little hope, precisely through his fineness in engineering, of surviving the hurly-burly of post-grouping life. Whitelegg's major contribution, his monstrous 4-6-4 tanks, was equally ill starred. In the event one solitary SW locomotive survived to pass into BR ownership. Though it was Whitelegg built, its design, as it happened, was Peter Drummond's. Even then it did not live long enough to carry its allotted BR number, 56905.

FINAL SOU' WEST VISITS

Although by March 1937 we knew the facts regarding G & SW survivors we could not resist paying another visit to Corkerhill. Call it nostalgia. Corkerhill still produced from somewhere two SW engines, both distinctive in their own rights. No 17820 was Drummond's first of eleven 2-6-0s he built, and, by equally happy coincidence, No 16900 proved to be the first of ten Drummond 0-6-2 tanks added by Whitelegg in 1919. Her appearance was no different from that of her earlier sisters.

Still determined to prove something or other Adam and I indulged in the luxury of one final trip to Kilmarnock in September 1937. The running shed had little to offer beyond the usual

page 125   LNER No 6809 (ex-GNSR) was an unusual visitor to Dundee in August 1936

page 126   L<small>NER</small> Nos 9203 and 9304 at Polmont in May 1935

flush of 2Ps. Behind the shed, however, rusting and unkempt in appearance, lay a fragment of railway history: 14411 *Ben Loyal*, exactly as built by Peter Drummond in his Highland days. The Small Ben still possessed her original boiler, with safety valves on top of her dome, and not for many moons had we set eyes on the elegant smokebox wingplates she still sported.

Further along the line two very disconsolate machines sat in the works yard. Caley No 14433 not only looked seedy, the plating over her front buffer beam had already been partially stripped. St Rollox, we feared, would see no more of her. Behind loomed the shabby bulk of 14517, one of Drummond's second batch of G & SW 4-4-0s. She, too, had reached the end of the line. A sad way, alas, to bid farewell—but such was my last sight of a Glasgow & South Western locomotive.

'TIS FOLLY TO BE WISE

Shortly after the war I opted to try my fortunes south of the Tweed, and consequently found myself employed in the main London office of my bank. Within a year I gravitated to securities department, where in course of time I came to know my chief, David Manson, rather well. Mr Manson occupied a desk plumb in centre of the department, and during a busy day's work it was normal practice for me, and many others, to whizz back and forth past this desk.

One day a book lay there. This in itself was hardly an unusual circumstance, and I must have passed by several times before I realised with a jolt that its dust cover bore a full-coloured illustration of one of the beautiful 4-6-0s James Manson built for the Sou' West around 1903. At the time I may say the intriguing coincidence of names struck me more forcibly than any consideration as to why a book on Scottish railways should be lying there at all.

The afternoon wore on, the book lay undisturbed, and each voyage I made past the desk added picquancy to what I conceived to be a rum situation indeed. Once or twice Mr Manson, who, I think, was aware of my interest in railways, glanced up quizzically as I passed, all but tempting me to blurt out there and then the secret I hugged to my breast. The longer the book remained on the desk, the more difficult I found it to restrain myself. Latterly, so great was the strain, I simply had to succumb.

My chief was busy, and I did not feel justified in disturbing him on what was largely a personal matter. I therefore approached a senior colleague who acted as his right-hand man. 'Do you think', I breathed confidentially, 'Mr Manson could possibly be aware that the green locomotive on the cover of his book was designed by a gentleman called—James Manson?' I stood back to await developments.

My colleague at least did not waste my time, but looked up lackadaisically from the stock prices he was checking.

'He should be', he observed drily. 'James Manson was his uncle.'

II

More Sheds

W I T H railways, as with everything else, the unexpected has a
habit of providing incidents which freeze as perfect cameos in the
memory. A case in point was a visit I made to Tay Bridge shed in
August 1936. Lodged at Perth one fine Sunday morning I
suddenly conceived the notion of visiting Dundee.

Fortune must have smiled upon my decision. Even as I
approached the shed *Dandie Dinmont*, on the brink of leaving,
paused long enough for me to set my camera and add an original
Scott to my collection. Next came a look at the sleeping inhabitants.
A class C 0-6-0 lay half in, half out of the shed; but by her side,
basking full in the sun, an infinitely more enticing prospect
presented itself—2564 *Knight of Thistle*, green, elegant and
beautifully poised.

Anxious to profit from the warm sunlight I stepped back
slowly and was concentrating on my view-finder, when a hint
appeared that another locomotive peeped from behind the
Pacific. First things first, I decided, and refused to be distracted
until my shot of the Gresley was complete. Then, calmly winding
my film, I walked on—into possibly the most thoroughgoing
surprise of my career. The other locomotive turned out to be a
Great North of Scotland 4-4-0: 6909, class D41! But *why*—at
Dundee! I shall never know. The shed by now was deserted, and
there was not a soul about I might have questioned.

Having exhausted the subjects immediately in view I moved
on, much cheered, to examine a few dead locos round the side.
Nothing much there of interest, it seemed. An NB J35 headed

the procession, followed by a J39. Then came another super-heater; but behind her, last in line, lurked one final surprise—ex-GE 4-6-0, class B12, No 8531! The great black bulk of this unexpected visitor was not rendered any more handsome either, I recall, by the clumsy feed water-heater apparatus she wore aloft.

So ended my one and only visit to Tay Bridge. For a smallish shed it had proved to be quite an establishment. Memories of that delightful day have remained with me since, with perhaps one minor blemish to cause me concern. It will be appreciated I had no option but to photograph 8531 in situ. Unfortunately, someone had dumped 2 tons of coal, albeit neatly bagged, right beside her. A delicate problem is involved. Dare I publish the result, I have often asked myself, without some Sassenach glee-fully assuming that this represented normal coaling procedure in the Frozen North?

EASTFIELD SHED, GLASGOW

A year earlier, in June 1935, Adam and I had carried out a memorable swoop on Polmadie and Eastfield sheds. Polmadie had been a little disappointing, in that we left there rich in haul of numbers but, photographically speaking, somewhat under-exposed, but we need not have fretted. Eastfield was going to do handsomely by us before the day was out.

Here in one large bustling depot NB engines of almost every existing class paraded themselves. Apart, possibly, from the GE shed at Stratford I had never seen such a wealth of native types shelter under one roof. Ex-NB passenger types proliferated. Even *Midlothian* was there, to represent a rapidly dwindling class of Reid Atlantic, and she was well supported by Scotts and Glens.

It was unnamed NB 4-4-0s, however, which revealed Eastfield's true worth. Drummond 4-4-0s had vanished within a year or so of grouping, but engines by his successor, Matthew Holmes, were still at work, albeit in rebuilt Reid form. No 9217, a superb example of Holmes's class M, now LNER class D31, awaited us. 6ft 6in coupled, the class was built in three series over the years 1884–99. The locomotive we now looked at belonged to the

second series. Typical of Eastfield variety, only a stone's throw
away 9382, one-time class K, now D33, sat quietly out of action
by an old coaling stage. A 6ft version of the original Scotts, this
was one of Reid's second Intermediates, *c* 1910. Only a dozen
were built, but their willingness to handle any kind of traffic
endeared them to NB hearts.

The next unnamed NB 4-4-0 to come our way looked very
spruce as she backed on to the turntable at Eastfield. From the
presence on her smokebox of a dainty black and white board,
inscribed 'Glasgow', we deduced she must have come in off West
Highland duty. Later, when we had time to consult our stock-
book, we got quite a shock to discover we had, in fact, photographed No 9695, sole representative of class D36.

There was indeed much more to her than met the eye.
Originally she was one of twenty-four Holmes-built engines
brought into service by the NB when their West Highland line
was opened in 1894; but alone of her class she was rebuilt along
Reid lines in 1919, and was specially reclassified D36 when taken
over by the LNER in 1923. Of her compatriots, meanwhile, seven
entered grouping in original form as class D35. All perished by
the end of 1924, leaving this one old lady to relish her charmed
existence. That she did too; for next time I saw her, again at Eastfield, in 1937, she was queueing patiently behind a Gresley
Pacific, waiting her turn to slip under the coaling tower, and still
looked not a whit out of place. By the time she was pensioned off
in 1943 she had only just failed to complete fifty years' service.

Eastfield was equally generous in the matter of NB tanks. At
one end of the shed, fairly bursting with pride, as befitted an
engine returned freshly painted from Cowlairs, 9861 had no
intention of being overlooked. Still, here was no ordinary 0-6-2
tank, for she was one of the celebrated half-dozen built in 1909
expressly to assist trains up Cowlairs bank. To us that day she
looked good enough for another twenty-five years on the incline.
Not far away lay No 9921, a 0-6-2 tank of later vintage, lifeless
and so inconspicuous, half under the shadow of a bridge, as to
warrant little attention normally. Our eyebrows shot up, however, at the sight of twin brass-columned safety valves on top of

her dome. Now why, we wondered, should a locomotive built late in Reid's career revert to Matthew Holmes's old practice? We had no idea, and intrigued by the paradox I took a precautionary picture.

Years later the explanation which came my way revealed closer links between the two tanks than we had imagined. While Reid's first six class A tanks were turned out with safety valve on dome, he switched to smaller closed-top domes when the class was later augmented. The six banking prototypes acquired new boilers in due course, but normal practice saw to it that old boilers fit to be reconditioned were not thrown away, and one or two of the originals, complete with safety valve on dome, moved subsequently round other locos of the same class. The odds, therefore, that 9921 that Saturday afternoon may have been sporting 9861's original boiler were no longer than one in six. A small, but intriguing, thought.

Another tank, 9823, one of forty utility 0-6-0s constructed by Holmes in 1900, was shed pilot for the day. Occasionally, as a variation from scuttling about the yard, she dived into the shed itself. Once she reappeared with *Baillie Macwheeble* on tow, and deposited the giant Director on an adjacent road before hopping back inside to attend to two more inmates, which she obligingly proceeded to haul outside, well clear of the murky shed environment. Delighted to take advantage of the shed pilot's diligence we followed the procession up the yard, cameras in hand.

The tiniest member of the party was 9237, one of Reid's little dock shunters, bearing an NB plate which advised she was class F, while her LNER front buffer beam cheerfully insisted she was class J88. Her much sturdier companion—class A, or N15, again according to preference—was No 9071, one of thirty-one Reid 0-6-2 tanks added by the LNER after grouping. Exactly like 9921, except for that enigmatic safety-valve arrangement. They made a handsome pair and our inclination to rest our legs awhile and nibble a sandwich over the view was only thwarted by the even more fetching appearance of *The Pirate* as the Scott emerged fully groomed from the shed, ready to take up whatever duties lay ahead. What sturdy busy engines these Scotts were! An hour later she pounded past Eastfield at the head of a Thornton express.

By then we had been up and down the shed area several times, adding photographic trophies to our day's haul. No 9053, one of the NB's first thirty Atlantic tanks, posed for us, then gave way to 9143, a superheated J37 0-6-0. We had hoped to catch one of the later superheated 4-4-2 tanks, class C16, which did much of the running around Helensburgh and points west, but the only representative on the premises, No 9512, remained rooted inside the shed. Then *Westmorland* and *Wandering Willie* emerged, coupled together. An interesting pairing, and we raced across to investigate. Despite the Shire's immaculate green livery, old black *Willie*, we were pleased to note, still looked quite a flyer. Adding still further to Eastfield's prodigious variety *Cicero* wandered next upon the scene, moving gracefully about the yard as only a Gresley Pacific can. Hard on her heels 626, a Gresley-built J50 0-6-0 tank, drifted in from Cadder.

Here was a heaven-sent camera opportunity, for usually these locos were to be seen only from a passing train as they laboured in the marshalling yards. The class, a mixture of new and rebuilt locomotives, was developed by Gresley in his early LNER days from an earlier GN prototype. A highly successful design, a handful of them had somehow found their way to Glasgow. As happened often in LNER days, clusters of numbers had been allocated from the former NE range. The Cadder engines, for instance, were all numbered in the 600 region.

For my part I found their GN appearance most attractive. The Ivatt chimney and large matching dome seemed well balanced by the neat rounded cab. A striking feature of their design, and one really audacious to NB eyes, was the manner in which the side-tanks had been extended to the smokebox and sloped neatly in front to permit unfettered vision through large spectacle cab-glasses. A cavity cut from the tank immediately over the leading wheels, introduced to facilitate front-end accessibility, added a final debonair touch to what seemed to me to be a highly sophisticated design.

To complete a stunning Gresley hat trick *Loch Laidon*

rumbled in, fresh from West Highland freight duties. She was, of course, one of the K2 2-6-0s built between 1918 and 1921 which Gresley sent north, with boiler mountings duly cut down, to operate so successfully between Glasgow and the West Highlands. Finally, even after fatigue and impending dusk had persuaded us to turn our steps homeward, Eastfield threw in a parting shot by sending a GE B12 4-6-0 and *Lady of the Lake* careering past us, coupled tender to tender. Later that evening we calculated our gains, and discovered that of twenty-one classes of ex-NB locomotive still on LNER books, no fewer than sixteen had come our way that wonderful afternoon.

Flushed beyond recall by our success at Eastfield, Adam and I began to let our gaze wander. It alighted on Aberdeen. Ferryhill, *Kittybrewster*—why not! Rash thinking this, for we were committed to a joint excursion Londonwards in the autumn, and funds were running low. But Midsummer madness won, and within days the requisite shed permits were in our hands.

JOURNEY TO ABERDEEN

The Compound which bustled briskly into Larbert that morning in July 1935 matched our own mood pretty well. Adam and I had been up practically since dawn, and unwilling to wait for Grahamston's first connection to the north had walked the 3 miles to Larbert station. We were in a hurry to get to the Granite City! The Compound certainly did not hinder us, but took us all the way in a fine spirited lift which confirmed the high opinion we already held of her species. An hour from Larbert, Perth South shed's locomotive ranks gleamed at us through fine drizzle, with never a dash of crimson to relieve the gloom. North of Perth whatever was going on at the Highland shed was carefully shielded, as usual, from main-line observation. The Compound addressed herself cheerfully enough to the 90 miles which still separated her and Aberdeen. Looking out from our rain-stained windows I confess Adam and I were finding it difficult to match her exuberance.

With tales of the Great Races to the North in mind my father had warned me to look out for Kinnaber Junction. Unfortunately the dear chap omitted to add that, unlike Carlisle, NB running powers into Aberdeen commenced 35 miles (!) south of the city. I leaned out at what I deemed to be a judicious distance south of Aberdeen—and was still peering earnestly for Kinnaber Junction when Ferryhill shed loomed up on the horizon! As I had obtained shed permits from LNER sources I suppose it had not occurred to me to wonder where exactly the LMS kept their engines. Certainly I was blissfully unaware that only two sheds in the country harboured locomotives belonging to rival companies. One was Ferryhill, the other Fratton, where engines of the LSW and LB & SC kept scrupulously to their own 'halves'. Now I braced myself to sail observantly past Ferryhill; and nearly fell to the carriage floor at the sight of NB and Caledonian locomotives sheltering snugly *under one roof*!

Shocked to the core I do not think I uttered one word the rest of the way into Aberdeen. Adam, unworried by NB pedigree, took advantage of my silence to calculate that as Ferryhill seemed a goodly step from the city, and he had seen nothing there of consequence in passing, any spare time we had in Aberdeen would best be spent pursuing Great North objectives. Shell shocked still by the heresy I had just witnessed I was in no condition to offer resistance.

ABERDEEN JOINT STATION

I suppose really we expected too much from our trip to the north. Great railway stations which play host to a variety of companies have a fascination all their own; but Aberdeen could never have been a Carlisle, much less a York. It soon became obvious that GN's activity hinged entirely on the frequency of trains to and from the south. Local passenger traffic was moderate in character, freight traffic negligible, and one could see why the GN, an active economical little concern at all times, perceived no need to vary their longstanding practice of building only 4-4-0s where tender locos were concerned. 6ft 1in driving wheels for passenger work, 5ft 7½in for mixed traffic. It made sense. So, too, did their design. The first GN engine to cross our path looked to our eyes more like a scale model, so trim was she, and such a charmer. We had gone up to see our Compound disengage, and there, standing light, facing that impressive gully of overbridges and gantries which so characterises the northern exit from Aberdeen, was No 6847 *Sir David Stewart.*

To young men weaned on the rugged bluntness of NB and Caledonian locomotive design the appearance of the little D40 posed a tantalising enigma. Built by Pickersgill in 1920, to 1899 specifications, her boiler was commensurately low, her chimney and dome both shapely and tall. Her safety valves were partly enclosed, as was the fashion of our native breeds, by a low flat cover; but her roomy double-windowed cab, with its roof ventilator, spoke of NE influence. Her tender could easily have been borrowed from an NB locomotive; yet the neat nameplate she bore was utterly alien to normal Scottish practice. At running-plate level the elegant sweep of her splashers and the wheel symmetry below took us back to more spacious days of Pollitt and Johnson. In the gentle light of the sun which had by now dared to assert itself she looked, we thought, a very lovely object indeed.

So far, so good. Once our initial excitement subsided there arose the vexation of deciding when we could leave the station to snatch a bite to eat. 'Now', opined Adam, and off we flew. Never were sandwiches and lemonade consumed more quickly; but, at least, our alacrity on returning to base earned prompt reward in the shape of another D40, 6848 *Andrew Bain,* drawn up ready to leave at the head of a local train. The way her black paint shone she could not have been long out of Kittybrewster shops.

Once she had gone peace descended, until about 1pm when impending departures at both ends of the station had us galloping up and down platforms. No 14637, a Caley class 60, slipped in (from Ferryhill!) to take up position at the head of the 1.5pm express to Glasgow Buchanan Street. Next to the engine was one of the Caley's celebrated maroon straw-boarded Pullman cars. Meanwhile, something about the 4-6-0 troubled us as she backed in.

Ah, her chimney! In place of her normal impressive-looking, one-piece Pickersgill chimney the one she bore was jointed in McIntosh fashion. It's interesting how one such detail quite

altered her appearance. Once we had seen the Caley off we switched to the northern end of the station, where yet another D40—this time unnamed, being of an earlier batch—reported in to handle the 1.30 stopping train to Inverurie. Typical of what we were beginning to appreciate were GN standards she shone like a button.

KITTYBREWSTER SHED

Again calm settled over the station. Adam consulted timetables and decided now was the time to make a dash for Kittybrewster. More surprises, for here awaited us the first Scottish shed we had ever seen remotely resembling a roundhouse (I discount, of course, the tiny refuge for saddletanks at St Margarets). We paused to register appropriate wonder, though the contents themselves were our real concern. One or two 4-4-0s lying inside the shed defied our cameras. Outside, in the yard, an interesting quartet more than compensated.

An ever-popular Scottish type, thanks to the Drummond influence, No 6888, one of nine 0-4-4 tanks designed by Johnson in 1893, now LNER class G10, had smaller driving wheels than her NB and Caledonian sisters. This appeared to give her an abnormally long wheelbase. She seemed to me half GC, half Midland in bearing. Next to her, both surprise and contrast, an ex-GE 2-4-2 tank, 7236, class F4, looked quite Scottish in her sturdiness. No stovepipe, but a pleasant long-shaped LNER chimney. Operating conditions on the Great North must have possessed some affinity with those in East Anglia, for not long after we heard of Holden 4-6-0s, with original boiler and Belpaire firebox, working successfully in the Aberdeen area. If nothing else I imagine the two regions shared a joint paucity of large turntables.

In some respects the third engine in the yard was the scoop of the day. Certainly we had never seen an 0-4-2 tank before. Manning Wardle supplied four such to the GNS in 1913, and here was No 6832. We were fortunate, for normally these engines spent their days round Aberdeen docks. A tidy little engine, we thought, but, where pedigree was concerned, very much of an odd man out. The sole tender loco in the yard turned out to be 6897, class D41, one of thirty-two Johnson built in 1893–8. Not quite so intriguing, we thought, as the D40, but I dare say her absence of name may have jaundiced us.

By late afternoon we had thoroughly explored the Kittybrewster seam and were beginning to think in terms of returning home, for we planned to complete the round trip to Falkirk via the Tay and Forth Bridges. It was well we got back to Aberdeen when we did—for who should arrive at the head of the *Aberdonian* but Gresley's mighty new Mikado, *Earl Marischal*?

What a sight! Built late in 1934 with normal valve gear, as opposed to *Cock o' the North*'s Lentz poppet valves, she differed in other respects from her illustrious sister; for she bore no feed water heater on her running plate, and additional smoke deflectors had been superimposed on her sleek streamlined front end. It was remarkable how such a powerful engine as she contrived to display a smooth uncluttered exterior. Doubly ironic, too, that she and her sisters proved too strong ultimately for the redoubtable tasks they were set. Despite failing light Adam snapped her as she chuffed gently back towards Ferryhill, her day's work done. A fitting conclusion to an interesting day, we decided; and turned away to seek our train for Dundee and parts south.

MOTHERWELL SHED

The urge to set foot on further virgin territory prompted Adam and I to visit Airdrie and Motherwell's Caledonian sheds in August 1936. Airdrie was smaller than we expected, but prospects looked better at Motherwell. Even as we reached the shed entrance a Horwich Mogul clanked by. Rather impulsively I raised a cheer, whereupon Adam counselled me severely against over optimism. As further evidence of a busy railway scene unfolded itself, however, I noticed his camera came out sharply enough.

Within ten minutes the two of us could have been found staring as if transfixed at something we had never seen before—a Caledonian 2-6-0. A second Horwich loco, jammed between Caley tender engines, had caught our attention, and as Adam shaped up to photograph her I wandered on—to find the next locomotive in line was McIntosh built all right, but hardly the 0-6-0 I had casually assumed her to be. Frantic signals brought Adam along to share my excitement. No 17800, burnished as if about to take over a London express, was in splendid condition. In typically Caley fashion she disdained to wear a number plate in front, but some enthusiast had taken the trouble, nevertheless, to outline her shed code plate carefully in white.

It was odd, but quite a few of McIntosh's larger locomotives possessed this deceptive habit of looking very much like their lower orders. Had not the discovery of the 2-6-0 alerted us we might conceivably have missed what was to be the crowning event of the day. For the dumpy tank engine which stood right at the end of an adjacent line of locomotives could easily have been bye-passed on a blazingly hot afternoon as just another McIntosh class 3 0-6-0. It was, in fact, a rare piece: 16950, first of five 0-8-0 tanks introduced by him in 1903. At grouping they had been allotted numbers 16500–05, but these were changed in 1926 to make room for the Jinties the LMS were pouring out. Considering all five 0-8-0s went to the scrapyard between 1932 and 1939, and we never saw a second one, our chance visit to Motherwell proved more fortuitous than we had any right to expect. Certainly I know Adam and I got home that night happy as sandboys; delighted to have exchanged 40 miles of strenuous cycling for two new Caledonian types. A naïve activity for grown young men, it must seem to some nowadays. But there—life, bless it, was like that in those days.

LAST OF THE WHEATLEYS

Hopes that a further visit to Eastfield might yield a second hoard of treasure were, of course, futile from the start. We knew it, but optimism and the element of surprise formed a large part of the railway enthusiast's morale in those days. Off went our application.

In the event it was Eastfield's neighbour which provided the prize of the day. We arrived at Cowlairs to find the strangest of visions lined up outside the adjacent locomotive works. The locomotive, an 0-6-0, was obviously vintage NB, but the visual effect it produced was one almost of discomfort. At first glance one suspected the driving wheels were too large for the remainder of the engine; or, alternatively, that the chimney and boiler mountings were disproportionately small. It took second thoughts to decide the latter was the true source of uneasiness. She was, in fact, No 10206, a 5ft 1in Wheatley veteran, built at Cowlairs sometime between 1867 and 1875.

Quite a history lay behind her, for although thirty-seven of the class survived grouping in 1923 soon all but this one old warrior had perished. No 10206 lingered stubbornly on, working quietly amongst the brick yards at Kipps, where one low bridge she had to slither under daily compelled the LNER to fit a modern chimney and dome to her comparatively puny boiler; sophisticated adornments which we could see for ourselves contrasted oddly with a shaped Stirling cab and early Victorian tender. The sight of her in such sombre surroundings convinced us she was paying her last visit to Cowlairs; and surely enough that same month LNER class J31 came to an end with her withdrawal. We considered ourselves very fortunate to have caught her.

ST ROLLOX LOCOMOTIVE WORKS

Still in 1937, and with the latter sentiment firmly in mind, the LMS, we next resolved, should receive some extra attention. Applications sent off included a request to visit St Rollox locomotive works in September of that year.

Apart from the pleasantly surprising discovery in the paintshops of the Caley single wheeler, newly decked in full company regalia, the works themselves held little of fresh interest for us. Outside, though, in the locomotive yard a vastly different tale lay waiting to be told.

As we emerged out under a leaden sky from the workshops door we were confronted by a forlorn-looking Drummond 0-6-0. She had about her an air of walking wounded, but by her side, looking much more prosperous, and glowing weirdly in the Glasgow half light, stood No 14684 *Duncraig Castle*. So fresh was she from the shops she and her tender had not yet been reunited.

Now, to my eyes at least, a Highland Castle never failed to look other than mournful, but this one might have been prepared for some solemn state occasion, so funereal was the shining black unlined livery the Caley shops had thought fit to lavish on her. Her brasses had been brightly polished; so, too, was a thin copper pipe which looped from her Westinghouse pump to run along the underside of her boiler before disappearing into her smokebox. Thoroughly foxed, Adam and I stood there for ten minutes, just gazing at this strange object. At one stage my friend opened his mouth to make some comment, but none emerged. Eventually came our opinion. With paintwork like that, we reckoned, even *Duncraig Castle* should be safe from the breakers' hands for a week or two. As it happened, she was the last Castle we were ever to see.

On we strolled, in no great hurry, content to pursue a leisurely inspection of the locomotive yard beyond, where, we could see, at least two columns of lifeless locomotives awaited our attentions. Ah, me, how simply in those days railway excitement could explode! We had hardly progressed fifty yards before hints appeared that St Rollox had further surprises in store. What on earth! With comical rapidity our respective strides smartened into something resembling a gallop. Heavens, look! *Two* new Highland types, just aching to be harvested!

First in view, 14422 *Ben-a-Chaoriunn*, looking uncannily like a LSW engine, as did most of Peter Drummond's later designs, came our way as a particularly inspired piece of good fortune. Like the Caley 0-8-0 tanks the first of her class disappeared in 1932, and here, just in time, was the sole survivor of six. Not a handsome engine, by a long chalk, but at least we had caught a Big Ben.

The second discovery was hardly as critical, for in the event locos of her class lived on to 1952. But to us at the time she was no less welcome. We had, in fact, assumed her to be a Clan; until a second look at her driving wheels, and a check on her barely decipherable number, 17953, jolted us into realising we were gaping at our first Clan Goods. The Cumming hallmarks were there, but it was illuminating to see how, by adding 6ft drivers

141

and softening a rather stubby front end, the designer had gone on to create real beauty with his express version, the Clan.

Memories of yet a third Highland prize that day at St Rollox floated to the surface in odd circumstances many years later. Looking back now I recall our joy when, down below in a lower-level yard, we spotted a Barney 0-6-0, one of a dozen built for the Highland by Drummond between 1900 and 1907. But for her original Drummond boiler, with twin brass-columned safety valve on top of her dome, she could easily have been overlooked as just another Caley Jumbo. Great, then, was my frustration when I developed the film, only to find that particular negative had fogged badly in one corner. Disgustedly I threw it aside as useless. Thirty years later, when preparing this book, I stumbled across the negative quite by accident, and anxious to refresh my memory from any available source I prepared a print therefrom.

The result is not only interesting, it reminds me yet again of the fallibility of human memory. For much of what I see on the print had, in fact, escaped my recollection. In the foreground appears the Barney we coveted. Behind her lurks a Compound, while on an adjacent road can be seen a Stanier MT 4-6-0. In front of the Stanier appears a Highland Loch, and evidence of a second. The third, and final, row consists of an LMS Standard 0-6-0, a G & SW Drummond 4-4-0, and what is almost certainly the tender of a third Loch. Quite a group.

Now that steam has gone I look at the picture from time to time, think of the appetite such an ensemble would now create amongst railway lovers—and can only marvel how innocently we viewed it all in 1937.

English immigrants: (*above*) LNER No 7347 (ex-GER) at Falkirk
Grahamston in April 1935; (*below*) LNER No 3064 (ex-GNR) at
Haymarket in August 1936

page 144
(*above*) LNER No 2511 *Silver King* at Haymarket in August 1936;
(*below*) LNER No 2796 *Spearmint* holds the stage as she glides into
Waverley station to take over the *Flying Scotsman* in August 1931

12

Thoughts—Sombre and Otherwise

FIRST intimation of railway mortality, as it were, came my
way when I was very young. I was on top of Springfield footbridge
one summer evening, and had just watched the Greenhill leave
when a small group further up the yard caught my attention. Three
or four railwaymen were propelling a hand trolley in my direction, and seemed to be doing so with exaggerated care. The reason
for such gentleness became apparent as they approached; for on
the trolley, covered by a dark blue railwayman's coat, lay a man.
I remember being shocked, and saddened, by the sight of that
white face. An ambulance appeared, and stationed itself in
readiness by the level-crossing gates; but long before the delicate
operation arose of transferring the injured man from his rough
resting place I had fled for home, frightened and sickened by my
unwonted initiation into the facts of railway life.

Next morning, when my father came off duty I overheard him
mention to my mother that a shunter colleague had met with an
accident at Springfield yard. Despite lowered voices I gleaned
that the poor chap had lost a leg, and had died before reaching
hospital. Obviously it had not occurred to my father that I might
know anything of the fatality, for nothing more was said. I wanted
badly to tell him what I had seen—but the memory of that
shocked face on the trolley disturbed me in a way I had never
known before, and prompted me to hold my peace.

Luckily enough, during the course of his long railway career
my father was spared serious injury. But his job was a dangerous
one and even an intelligent practitioner such as he could hardly

hope to escape unscathed. One morning, I well remember, I woke early and in the gas light of our tiny cottage perceived him, face drawn with pain, gently bathing the badly crushed index finger of his right hand. Whilst on duty he had slightly miscalculated the use of his shunting pole, and this was the consequence. Later that morning he attended the doctor, had the wound stitched and dressed, and quite as a matter of course resumed normal railway duties that same evening.

Another time he booked off at Polmont late one stormy night and, coming away from the yard, fell headlong into an engine ashpit. With ice on the ground and snow falling heavily a man in such straits might easily have been excused had he sought refuge in the warmth of the yard bothy. My father elected to carry on. After stumbling in pitch darkness down 5 miles of permanent way he eventually arrived home in the early hours, bruised from head to foot by his fall, shocked, and in such a state of exhaustion as to bring tears to my mother's eyes. By sheer chance his next duty, the Carlisle, offered 16hr respite. Never doubting for a moment his capacity to recover quickly he rested as long as he could, rose at the appropriate hour, and set off, shaken still, to take charge of his beloved Carlisle. Like so many more of his contemporaries his reserves of physical strength were nothing abnormal. The secret lay in heart and loyalty.

Nevertheless, with railwaymen such was the nature of their jobs disaster loomed large in their lives. My father was no pessimist, but from earliest boyhood contacts with him I learned certain calamities had seared themselves indelibly on his mind. The Tay Bridge disaster, though it occurred long before *he* joined the NB, seemed somehow to have acquired the characteristics of a personal affront. The Quintinshill tragedy of 1915 grieved him deeply and long. The Caley were the sufferers on this occasion, but it hardly required an act of imagination, even on my small part, to understand why a disaster costing 227 lives should strike hard at the heart of any railwayman. It was, perhaps, as well he had no way of knowing equally dreadful things would happen at Harrow before his days in this world were over.

GENERAL STRIKE—1926

In railway writings one often reads of the author's participation as 'volunteer' driver or fireman in the General Strike of 1926. There was, of course, another side. My father took part in the strike. He was a sincere Union man and would never have dreamed of dissenting once a collective decision was made. At the time I was only nine, so I cannot profess to have followed the political implications of the strike. But even at that age I recall the equanimity with which my parents approached the anxiety of losing our family livelihood, and I can still hear the names of Cook, Snowden, Jim Thomas and Ramsay Macdonald being bandied over my head; the latter two with increasing bitterness as men began to realise their cause was lost.

I remember, too, Falkirk's deserted streets that first morning; just like a Sunday, except for the tensions which smouldered beneath the surface. The bad railway accident at St Margarets, and the (potentially worse) derailment at Cramlington which followed, were not to my father's liking, and drew little comment from him, but he was man enough, and wise enough, to understand the passions which racked thousands of his colleagues. One final memory lingers, that of the mass return once the struggle was over. I saw my father go back, and understand now the conflict of emotions which must have played within him; wounding regret at the failure of the strike, inevitable sense of relief at returning to work, and, above all I like to think, a feeling of pride at having stood by his workmates in a desperate bid for social justice. Men like him need no apology.

RAILWAY COLLEAGUES AND CHARACTERS

Dangers, disasters or no, railwaymen coped, and still retained faith and a sense of humour in their daily workings. My father at all times held his colleagues in high esteem. I do not doubt that those I had the good fortune to meet represented a fair cross section. Some were fine men, others were 'characters'. Others still combined both qualities; and of these none more colourful came my way than Tom Wilson.

Tom Wilson was a fellow goods guard at Polmont, and over

the years a lasting friendship and respect had ripened between him and my father. This in itself was interesting, for to all appearances the two men were as poles apart, Tom being as voluble and impulsive as my father was quiet and deliberate. Tom was the epitome of cheerfulness and seemed to possess an inexhaustible talent for bubbling his way through life, though I doubt if many men displayed a greater capacity for involving themselves in argument en route! He was, too, a born raconteur and any story he cared to tell clothed itself automatically in a wealth of dramatic detail. Tom's versions of some of his more elaborate shunts convulsed Polmont bothy many a time.

One tale, treasured at Polmont, of Tom 'at work' concerned a shunt he was called upon to execute at a local foundry, the object of the exercise being to deposit empty wagons in a loading shed therein. Tom, it appears, duly arrived with his train of empties in early morning darkness and with little more than usual difficulty lined everything up, right on target. Satisfied eventually that all was in order he flashed his green lamp. The train engine dutifully reversed—and within seconds the quiet morning air was assailed by the most appalling shrieks of rending timber. He had only forgotten to open the shed door.

Lesser mortals might reasonably have panicked. Not Tom. Sizing up the situation fairly and squarely, and pausing only to switch his lamp glass to red, he strode out imperiously from the side of the train, waved his lamp forrard and, surrounded still by the awful sounds of timber in torment, issued what he considered to be requisite instructions to his near-demented train crew. 'Hold on!' cried Tom. 'I hear something crackin!'

Yet this delightful character possessed a rare talent which though valued highly by his workmates generated strangely little conceit within him. He made violins. His adolescence, it seemed, was spent in a far northern locality where fiddle making and playing were endemic, and when, like my father, Tom forsook the land to obtain the security of railway employment he brought his inherited skill with him. He and his family lived now in a modest house not far from Polmont shed and there his fiddle-making activities jostled amicably with his wife's cooking chores for possession of a small kitchen. His good lady, tiny and resilient, had a happily uncomplicated opinion of her husband; she *knew* he was wonderful. He was, in fact, a most fastidious craftsman, and any time one visited the Wilson menage fiddle necks, scrolls, backs and bellies, all beautifully fashioned from such pieces of wood as Tom could legitimately commandeer, hung in profusion from the kitchen walls.

Here, too, was the man to whom I owe much of the lifelong pleasure music making has given me, for it was his enthusiasm for the instrument plus my parents' typically Scottish resolution to advance their childrens' education that fired within my father a resolve to 'put' me to the violin at the tender age of eight. A rum decision, I thought at the time—for I was unaware I possessed any talent other than that for getting into mischief. Anyhow, up to Polmont I was conducted—to meet Tom Wilson.

I liked the man at sight. He might easily have been a character from Dickens. His head, shiny and bald, was flanked by twin patches of white, his cheeks glowed ruddy, a trimmed white military moustache bristled to order, and behind the steel-rimmed spectacles he affected twinkled the merriest pair of blue eyes I ever saw on a man. In a bid to underwrite my musical conversion he had even laid on a demonstration of violin duets by his two sons. One was left handed, I recall, and employed a fiddle specially made for him by his father. Neither was particularly gifted but there I sat, thoroughly awed, while two young men sawed vigorously and at opposing angles over my head. So proud was Tom of his two sons it would have been rank heresy on my part to have refused the challenge. Accordingly my hands were scrutinised and Tom's kind offer to lend me a half-sized instrument accepted. Fiddle, bow, case, even tutor were thrust upon me and, his heart filled by now to overflowing, my father escorted his precious cargo home, by bus.

Much to everyone's gratification musical progress was made. Tom was good enough later to lend me a three-quarter-sized violin and eventually came the great day when father and I called to buy a full-sized instrument. Unbeknown to me Tom had some time back spotted a likely piece of wood and had been engaged

THOUGHTS—SOMBRE AND OTHERWISE

for months making my new violin. It was a lovely instrument, golden in colour and nicely voiced. Ere long it helped me gain success at a local musical festival, and as a consequence I was invited to play at the winners' concert.

That night, as I stood on the platform re-performing my test piece, my heart went out to two men sitting a few rows back in the auditorium. On my father's face sat the slightly comical expression of one who was valiantly, however unsuccessfully, trying to conceal parental satisfaction. By his side, unashamedly transported by pride and pleasure, his face beaming like a full moon, sat dear Tom Wilson. The following year success again came my way. This time the elation of my two sponsors was no greater than mine when, as a reward, I was promised my first railway trip to Carlisle.

NB DRIVER

Another character, Driver Bartholomew, dwelt in a cottage at the end of our street. Friend and contemporary of my father he was big, barrel chested, and capable of looking quite fierce. In actuality he was the courtliest of men. He and I often used to pass each other on Falkirk's streets as he returned home from duty, but though I was well aware of his presence, the reverse, I fear, did not apply. He always reminded me of a great amiable bear as he strode along with tea can dangling from his fist. From first I knew him he was occupied solely on the local NB Grangemouth & Bo'ness branch service. Often at Grahamston I used to watch him when, having run round his train, he would ease his tank back on to his fireman who crouched between the tracks, ready to couple up. Then, having executed the gentlest of buffer contacts, he would settle down placidly to read a scrap of newspaper. Immensely strong I never saw anyone throw a heavy reverse lever with quite such nonchalance as he.

One day, a long time ago, when my family were on their way to Polmont for holiday, my father and he were chatting at Grahamston and Driver Bartholomew, noticing me peer into the cab, thrilled me immeasurably by inviting 'the laddie to jump in'. The laddie obeyed with alacrity and had his first experience of the warmth and wonder of an open locomotive firebox. For a few wild moments hopes were entertained that my driver friend might be induced to let me ride thus up to Polmont; but, of course, my father saw to it that I travelled in conventional fashion.

Some years later, when I was eleven, I had the good fortune to win a junior violin class at the local musical festival. In those days competition in such matters was keen, and local newspapers printed winners' photographs and made a fuss generally. A day or two later I was haring up Falkirk's main thoroughfare, solely intent on attending a cowboy film matinee, when without warning a large object planted itself firmly in my path. All I could see at eye level was a bulky dungaree-clad frame. I looked up. From a great height two blue eyes looked down. It was Driver Bartholomew. 'You're Peter Middlemass's laddie', he gruffed.

None too sure whether to regard this opening gambit as a challenge or an accusation I did my best to look non-committal, while my brain revolved frantically, searching for memories of any railway misdemeanour I might recently have committed. The conversation, meanwhile, resumed its one-way tenor.

'Tom Wilson tells me ye won the festival.' Ah-h! A slight exaggeration, perhaps, but enough to stop my brain revolving. Considerably relieved I made small modest noises. He listened politely, and as I petered into insignificance a ham-like hand descended on my shoulder. 'Stick in, laddie. Your father's very proud of ye!' Off he ambled, leaving all 4ft of me to swagger uptown, by now in such a state of euphoria at having been commended, much less spoken to, by an NB *engine driver* that had any pedestrian that afternoon been foolhardy enough to stay my progress to the cinema I am sure I should have shot from the hip first, and asked questions later.

FAREWELL TO THE NORTH BRITISH

I saw my last NB engine in April 1965, when I visited Scotland by car, and, reluctant to accept my brother's assurance that Polmont shed had been razed to the ground, insisted on taking a trip round my old haunts.

Polmont had gone all right. But Fouldubs lived on, and there, completely out of context amongst BR types in a Caley shed, an NB superheater, now No 64580, mouldered quietly in a siding, her career very obviously at an end. I photographed her and went back to my car, but even as I switched on the ignition I turned it off again—for memories were flooding back. For an hour or more, I suppose, I sat there, engulfed in a wave of nostalgia as an epoch slipped past in my mind's eye. Some day, I resolved, I must write about it, in an effort to convey to younger generations something of its charm.

Gone, too, were all the fine men I knew; my father with them— for at the ripe age of eighty-seven he passed on as cleanly and unfussily as any shunt he ever made. I remember the cold winter's day of his funeral. His sons and a friend or two were with him. Next to me as we lowered the bier into the ground stood John Swinton, a Polmont goods guard of later vintage who, trained initially by my father, had worshipped him ever since. Sensing the melancholy we all felt John spoke gently to me as we turned to go home.

'Never mind', he said. 'He was a grand railwayman.'

And you know, for the life of me, I cannot think what finer epitaph a man could ask for.

Index

INDEX OF LOCOMOTIVE TYPES

gill 0-6-0, 48, 60; McIntosh 2-6-0, 114, 138; Dunalastair 4-4-0, 23, 61, 66; McIntosh 4-4-0, 63, 67; Pickersgill 4-4-0, 61; 0-4-2, 28; Single-wheeler, 28, 112, 140; 0-8-0T, 139; 4-6-2T, 41; McIntosh 'Dock' 0-6-0T, 49; McIntosh 0-6-0T, 47, 49; McIntosh 0-4-4T, 15, 49; Balerno 0-4-4T, 100; 4-4-0T, 110

Ex-GN of s types:
D40, 136; D41, 129, 138; G10, 137; 0-4-2T, 137

Ex-Great Central types:
ROD 2-8-0, 109; J9 0-6-0, 44

Ex-Great Eastern types:
B12 4-6-0, 59, 130, 134; J69 0-6-0T, 44; F4 2-4-2T, 137

Ex-Great Northern types:
K2 2-6-0, 59, 134; D1 4-4-0, 60; N2 0-6-2T, 69, 91; J50 0-6-0T, 133

Ex-G & SWR types:
2-6-0, 117, 119, 124; Manson 0-6-0, 121; Drummond 4-4-0, 123, 127; 4-6-4T, 118; 0-6-2T, 77, 121, 124

Ex-Highland types:
Jones Goods, 104; Castle, 65, 109, 112, 120, 140; Clan, 64, 104, 110; Clan Goods, 141; River, 104, 106; Barney 0-6-0, 142; Loch 4-4-0, 106, 142; Small Ben, 109, 127; Big Ben, 141

Ex-LNWR types:
Claughton, 81; Prince of Wales, 82; Precursor, 82; Jumbo, 80

Ex-Midland types:
4-4-0, 78, 83

Ex-North British types:
J31, 140; J35, 45; J36, 44, 93; J37, 44, 133, 152; Atlantic, 29, 69, 82, 94, 110, 112; D25, 31, 60; D31, 130; D33, 131; D35, 131; D36, 131; Glen, 41, 52, 112; Scott, 41, 52, 91, 132; N14, 86; N15, 132; J83 0-6-0T, 86, 132; J88 0-6-0T, 93, 132; 4-4-2T, 46, 133; G9 0-4-4T, 46; Y9 0-4-0ST, 46, 99

Ex-North Eastern types:
Pacific, 30; Atlantic, 29, 52; 4-4-0, 81

INDEX

LMS types:

Royal Scot 4-6-0, 32, 50, 80, 113, 114; Stanier MT 4-6-0, 65, 66, 113; Jubilee 4-6-0, 114, 116, 119, 123; Horwich 2-6-0, 60, 65, 104, 110; Class 4F 0-6-0, 48, 60; Compound 4-4-0, 41, 50, 62, 65, 101, 116, 120, 134; 2P 4-4-0, 115, 119, 123; Dock Tank 0-6-0, 100

LNER types:

Pacific, 55, 68, 80; 2-8-2, 138; Sandringham 4-6-0, 58; J39, 130; K3, 43, 73; Director, 52, 56, 58, 69, 118, 134; Shire, 52, 58, 112, 133; Hunt, 59; 2-6-2T, 46